Persuasion

Persuasion: The Hidden Forces that Influence Negotiations represents the first book of its kind to package and present persuasion principles in an innovative, international, and interdisciplinary fashion.

This easy-to-understand book is the culmination of seminal research findings spanning across decades and disciplines – psychology, philosophy, negotiations, decision-making, logic, law, and economics, among others – from leading experts around the world. *Persuasion* provides a series of short, simple-to-use intellectual tools to go above and beyond merely describing "what to think" – but "how to think" in a persuasion, influence, and negotiation context – across a diverse array of disciplines, sectors, and situations from boardrooms to classrooms for the twenty-first century.

Jasper Kim, JD/MBA, is a lawyer, former investment banker, director of the Center for Conflict Management, and faculty at Ewha Womans University. He was a visiting scholar at Harvard University and Stanford University. Jasper Kim received negotiation training at Harvard Law School and graduate economics training at the London School of Economics. He has published in dozens of academic journals, consulted and trained leading global organizations, and has been featured in major media outlets, including the BBC, Bloomberg, CNBC, CNN, Forbes, and the *Wall Street Journal*. Learn more at jasperkim.com.

Routledge Focus on Business and Management

The fields of business and management have grown exponentially as areas of research and education. This growth presents challenges for readers trying to keep up with the latest important insights. Routledge Focus on Business and Management presents small books on big topics and how they intersect with the world of business research.

Individually, each title in the series provides coverage of a key academic topic, whilst collectively, the series forms a comprehensive collection across the business disciplines.

Management Accounting for Beginners
Nicholas Apostolides

Stories for Management Success
The Power of Talk in Organizations
David Collins

How to Resolve Conflict in Organizations
The Power of People Models and Procedure
Annamaria Garden

Branding and Positioning in Base of Pyramid Markets in Africa
Innovative Approaches
Charles Blankson, Stanley Coffie and Joseph Darmoe

Persuasion
The Hidden Forces that Influence Negotiations
Jasper Kim

For more information about this series, please visit: www.routledge.com/Routledge-Focus-on-Business-and-Management/book-series/FBM

Persuasion

The Hidden Forces that Influence Negotiations

Jasper Kim

Routledge
Taylor & Francis Group

LONDON AND NEW YORK

First published 2018 by Routledge

2 Park Square, Milton Park, Abingdon, Oxfordshire OX14 4RN
52 Vanderbilt Avenue, New York, NY 10017

Routledge is an imprint of the Taylor & Francis Group, an informa business

First issued in paperback 2019

British Library Cataloguing-in-Publication Data
A catalogue record for this book is available from the British Library

Library of Congress Cataloging-in-Publication Data
Names: Kim, Jasper, author.
Title: Persuasion : the hidden forces that influence negotiations /
    Jasper Kim.
Description: Abingdon, Oxon ; New York, NY : Routledge, 2018. |
    Series: Routledge focus on classical studies | Includes
    bibliographical references and index.
Identifiers: LCCN 2018002273 | ISBN 9780815361954 (hardback) |
    ISBN 9781351113717 (e-book)
Subjects: LCSH: Persuasion (Psychology) | Negotiation.
Classification: LCC BF637.P4 K476 2018 | DDC 153.8/52—dc23
LC record available at https://lccn.loc.gov/2018002273

ISBN: 978-0-8153-6195-4 (hbk)
ISBN: 978-0-367-37569-0 (pbk)

Typeset in Times
by Apex CoVantage, LLC

"How quick come the reasons for approving what we like"

Persuasion, Jane Austen

This book serves to empower ordinary people to do the extraordinary.

Contents

Foreword

People use persuasion every day. Persuasion occurs everywhere and anywhere – often hidden and invisible – from boardrooms to classrooms. It is the hidden ability to influence, induce, and incentivize people and situations.

Persuasion: The Hidden Forces That Influence Negotiations represents the first book of its kind to package and present persuasion principles in an innovative, international, and interdisciplinary fashion. This easy-to-understand book is the culmination of seminal research findings spanning across decades and disciplines – psychology, philosophy, negotiations, decision-making, logic, law, and economics, and others – from leading experts around the world.

Persuasion is presented in the form of eight hidden forces. Some hidden forces are "behavioral" hidden forces (based on our psychological influences, judgments, biases, and perceptions). The remaining hidden forces are "rational" hidden forces (based on our cognitive strategies, expectations, elements, and reasonings). These two big-picture hidden forces – behavioral and rational – oscillate between being solitary or complementary depending on the individual and context encountered. Individually and collectively, persuasion's hidden forces influence people and situations.

Much of the past academic literature in the field of persuasion and related sciences has presumed that individuals are rational choice actors. But does this assumption always hold true? Do individuals always use and apply rational choice – dutifully devoid of the seeming whims of emotion and other behavioral elements – in decision-making processes, actions, and outcomes?

Under rational choice theory (RCT) – colloquially referred to in this text as "Rationalists" – within and even beyond a persuasion context, individuals are always assumed to make informed decisions. Such decisions are presumed to have been made only after careful thought and dutiful deliberation of the probabilistic outcomes of all possible events – while internally weighing a mental scale that intimately calibrates the relative costs and benefits of each and every particular outcome – using all available information. From such

"Rationalist" lens, the actions of individuals are always "rational" in that individuals are in a constant pursuit of transitive logic that culminates in a choice or series of choices that serve to maximize utility. The concept of "utils" or "widgets" – using parlance from an imagined academic marketplace mind game composed of hypothetical actors, goods, and services – in the dominant fields of economics, political science, sociology, philosophy, and others has trickled down into other disciplines, including the field of persuasion. The Rationalists represent a dominant force in both academic and practitioner circles, which include heavyweight academicians such as Gary Becker of the University of Chicago, Milton Friedman of Stanford University, and Patrick Dunleavy of The London School of Economics and Political Science (LSE).

In a rebuttal to the Rationalists, a "behavioral" school of thought – colloquially referred to in this text as "Behavioralists" – has emerged that questions a bedrock foundation underlying much of the RCT-based academic literature. The behavioral school of thought essentially argues that individuals do not *always* act in the mode of *homo economicus*. Rather, the mind, including well-informed bright and beautiful minds, often take mental shortcuts to make complex and even simpler decisions rather than undergo the laborious process of finely calibrated, constant calculations and analyses to render each decision within the context of an individual's decision-making calculus. Such mental shortcuts – more formally referred to as "heuristics" – represent a means by which to cut through the seemingly daunting deluge of data that barrage individuals on a daily basis. The Behavioralists include scholars such as Robert Shiller of Yale University, Richard Thaler of the University of Chicago, and Daniel Kahneman of Princeton University.

Rather than persuade the reader what to think, the objective of this book, *Persuasion*, is to explain and analyze the basic bedrock tenets underlying both schools of thought – the Behavioralists and the Rationalists – within the overarching rubric relating to the field of persuasion. This methodology allows the reader to decide when each model works, and fails to work, in theory and practice. In other words, this book explains not just how individuals "ought" to behave as rational choice thinkers, but also how individuals "actually" do behave in certain, contextual circumstances because of behavioral and rational hidden forces.

Such two-tiered conceptual approach, including both Behavioralist and Rationalist frameworks, is unique and needed in our modern twenty-first century era of increasing complexity. After all, the world today is no longer composed of stark "black or white" binary realities, but rather, varying and discrete shades of gray. Such shades intricately or indirectly involve issues pertaining to peace, conflict, deal-making, and many other critical issues in between. In a world ranging from full trust to zero trust – from perfect information to highly imperfect information, and symmetrical power dynamics to asymmetrical power dynamics – the inclusion rather than exclusion of both the Rationalist and Behavioralist schools of thought will not just be absolutely advantageous, but also unabashedly and unequivocally necessary for practitioners, policy makers, academics, and students.

This book is divided into two thematic parts: *Behavioralists* (Part I) and *Rationalists* (Part II). As a brief caveat to dividing the book in this way, it should be noted and understood that chapters and core concepts discussed in one chapter may often link to other chapters of this book.

Persuasion's methodological style is to convey concepts in easy-to-understand short chapters (with each chapter containing core concepts). Such methodology wraps around and reflects the highly compressed, 24/7 demands and nature of working professionals, academics, and students today, who even as highly informed people, seek knowledge in the most user-friendly and succinct format possible. Each brief chapter essentially represents a short primer of specifically identified key frameworks taken from the relevant literature and applied cases.

Part I (Behavioralists) provides brief chapters related to the Behavioralist school of thought pertaining to persuasion. Specific chapter concepts include an overview and analysis of influences (cognitive influences that impact individual thinking), judgments (mental shortcuts made in decision-making), biases (behavioral tendencies in a persuasion context), and perceptions (relating to ethics, fairness, and other disciplines).

Part II (Rationalists) provides brief chapters related to the Rationalist school of thought pertaining to persuasion. Specific chapters and concepts include an overview and analysis of strategies (prisoner's dilemma, tit-for-tat, mutually assured destruction, dominant strategy, and bargaining zones), expectations (expected value and related frameworks in decision-making), elements (communication, relationships, interests, options, legitimacy, alternatives, and commitment underlying distributive and integrative bargaining models), and reasonings (logical structures in syllogistic argumentation and rhetoric).

Using both the Behavioralist and Rationalist lenses, this book's frameworks ultimately provide further clarity regarding many of the central questions underlying the principles of persuasion: What is the best "strategy" relating to persuasion? Are individuals always "rational" in persuasion and decision-making? And how do such persuasion principles shape the world today?

This succinct book's intent is not to provide "one-size-fits-all" answers within an expansive encyclopedic text. The objective of *Persuasion* is instead to provide a series of short, simple-to-use intellectual tools to go above and beyond merely describing "what to think" – but "how to think" in a persuasion, influence, and negotiation context – cutting across a diverse array of disciplines, sectors, and situations for the twenty-first century.

Part I

Behavioralists

Pride and prejudice

1 Influences

Invisible influences of persuasion

Influence

One of the most noted experts in the area of social psychology and influence is Robert Cialdini. Based on his research, Cialdini has proposed six specific principles of influence, which he argues serve as invisible influencers (Cialdini 1993).

Specifically, the six principles of influence are:

- Reciprocity
- Scarcity
- Authority
- Consistency
- Liking
- Consensus

The following section delves inside the six principles of influence.

The first principle of influence is reciprocity. Reciprocity reflects how certain individuals feel obliged to return to others what they have received first. If a friend or colleague gives a gift, then the recipient of such gift generally feels obligated to reciprocate in kind. Behavior linked to reciprocity may make intuitive sense to many people already. However, what is noteworthy in the relevant research findings conducted by Cialdini (1993) and others is the level or amount of reciprocity that is given back after something is received. In a series of studies involving customers in restaurants, giving a simple mint by a waiter increased tips by around 3 percent. When the amount was doubled to two mints, tips quadrupled (not just doubled) to 14 percent. Research also noted the impact of not just what amount was given, but how it was given. Specifically, when a waiter initially provided just one mint, then turned around and said, "For you nice people, here's another mint," tips surged to 23 percent (rather than doubling to 6 percent). Thus, the takeaways are, first, to initiate the giving; second, make such giving personalized to the parties at issue; and third, ensure that such giving is unexpected (that is, the recipient should gain a sense of specialized and personalized treatment) (Strohmetz, Rind, Fisher & Lynn 2002).

The second principle of influence is scarcity. When a good or service is viewed as scarce, then human behavior often desires more of such good or service (Novotney 2014). Such scarcity can appear in various written forms, such as with "limited edition," "first come, first serve," and "for a limited time only" branding. Even the threatened or actual banning of a particular item may trigger individuals to want more of a particular thing, perhaps out of fear of not having access to such opportunity in the future. The instant selling out of Nike Air Jordans or other coveted products is a form of scarcity, as are flash sales and pop-up stores, which often triggers individuals to want more of the thing perceived as scarce. This also conforms to the economic principle that "scarcity drives value up," as in the case of diamonds (which has a limited or set supply). Cialdini suggests that the scarcity principle should be augmented not only by communicating the benefits of having such perceived or actual scarce item, but also to demonstrate what is unique about the item or service in question, and what parties may lose as a result of not having such item or service (Cialdini 1993).

The third principle of influence is authority. It reflects the notion that individuals tend to follow the requests or recommendations of actual or perceived knowledgeable, credible experts. Signaling such authority can come in various forms, such as the displaying of academic diplomas by medical doctors. Separate from actual expert knowledge, even perceived, but not actual knowledge can trigger the authority principle. Studies found that individuals were more willing to give money to complete strangers if such strangers were simply wearing some kind of uniform (Bickman 1974). As a further example, many doctors wear stethoscopes even though their particular medical specialty often does not require using stethoscopes on a routine basis. Authority in the form of clothing must also be specific to the industry. Often wearing a suit and tie signaled authority and knowledge in the twentieth century. But today, in fields like technology and start-ups, wearing a suit and tie may have the opposite effect, while wearing jeans and a hoodie may instead reflect authority and expert knowledge.

The fourth principle of influence is consistency. In general, people were found to try to remain consistent with their past behavior. Based on this, a strategy of soliciting small initial concessions followed by larger subsequent concessions can be used in line with the consistency principle. As demonstration of the consistency principle of influence, a seminal study found a 400 percent increase over a control group in allowing large "Drive Safely" signs to be placed in front of individuals' homes simply because those same homeowners had allowed a postcard-sized sign indicating a similar message a few weeks earlier (Freedman & Fraser 1966). In sum, such commitments should be voluntary, active, and public, ideally in written form.

The fifth principle of influence is liking. Individuals generally were more likely to cooperate with persons they like. Specifically, such liking principle was a function of interacting with people who were viewed as most similar to the person in question, those who gave genuine compliments, and those who cooperated together toward similar goals. In a study involving online negotiations (e-negotiations) between two top-tier business schools, one group was told, "Time is money," and then, immediately began the negotiations. Meanwhile, a separate group was told to first take a few minutes to talk with their negotiation counterparty, emphasizing points of mutual similarity with one another (a form of social lubrication), followed only then by engaging in the negotiation at hand with the same party. In this latter group, 90 percent reached successful, negotiated outcomes worth 18 percent more to both parties compared with the group that was told to skip the small talk and enter straight into the negotiation (Morris, Nadler, Kurtzberg & Thompson 2002).

The sixth, and final, principle of influence is consensus. The consensus principle suggests that individuals often benchmark or reference the actions and behaviors of others to determine a particular course of future action or behavior, particularly in cases of uncertainty (Cialdini 1993). The consensus psychological phenomenon occurs in cases where no rational reason exists for such consensual action, such as when a group of bystanders collectively looks up toward the top of a tall building while standing on a sidewalk simply because others are doing the same thing. The work attire at various organizations also often reflect a very narrow band of clothing and hairstyles chosen by both men and women in a conscious or unconscious effort to conform to the consensus principle of influence.

In addition to Cialdini's findings, a plethora of other methods and techniques exist to get one individual to like another individual; these methods are discussed next.

Persuasion and self-focus

The persuasion and invisible influence of others is also, based on several studies, linked to steering a focus on or toward the other party.

In studies at Stanford University and the University of Arizona, participants preferred to be paired with other people who had aligned views. This may be because individuals may want to be perceived by others in a way that most closely conforms with the participants' own view of themselves (Robinson & Smith-Lovin 1992).

Other research conducted at Harvard University suggests that allowing individuals to talk about themselves increased an internal reward mechanism not too dissimilar from money, food, and sex (Tamir & Mitchell 2012). In this study, participants were placed in an fMRI machine to monitor their cognitive function. Activity in the brain region associated with reward and motivation were most active when participants shared information publicly about themselves.

Persuasion and influence are also based on the words individuals use to describe other people. In a published study, this "spontaneous trait transference" phenomenon applies in both positive and negative contexts. If positive language is used by a person to describe others, then others will tend to take a more positive view of that person. However, if negative language is used by a person to describe others, then others will tend to take a more negative view of such person (Skowronski, Carlston, Mae & Crawford 1998).

Revealing one's weaknesses to increase trust and likability was also confirmed by a study at the University of Texas, Austin. In the study, students who did well on a quiz but spilled coffee afterward were rated higher in likability compared who those who did not spill coffee. This phenomenon is known as the "pratfall effect," in which likability increases after mistakes are made. But this comes with a caveat: to create such perception, observers must first believe that such person is a competent person already (Aronson, Willerman & Floyd 1966). This effect is a version of the "stereotype content model," coined by psychologists at Princeton University, which proposes that individuals judge others based on the individual's level of warmth and competence (in this order) (Fiske 2013).

The simple act of smiling when focusing on others has also been shown to have a demonstrable effect in both in-person and virtual (online) contexts. A University of Wyoming study tasked nearly 100 undergraduate women with viewing photos of other women in (1) smiling, open-body positions; (2) smiling, closed-body positions; (3) not smiling, open-body positions; and (4) not smiling, closed-body positions. The photos with a woman smiling – regardless of body position – were viewed most favorably in the study (McGinley, McGinley & Nicholas 1978). In another study conducted at Stanford University and the University of Duisburg-Essen involving the online interaction among avatars, those online interactions involving avatars with bigger smiles recorded more positive experiences. Thus, in a persuasion context, smiling face-to-face both in a conference setting or through an online platform will tend to lead to higher likability rates and reviews compared with not smiling (Righi, Gronchi, Marzi, Mohamed & Viggiano 2015).

Persuasion and emotion

Persuasion is also shaped by perception based on an individual's state of emotion.

Before going further, stop reading. Next, think about what the reader focused on while reading up this point – perhaps it was the black letters written on the page? This may give a skewed sense and focus on the color black, when as the reader well knows after thinking about it, the page is composed mostly of the color white. Linked to this focus and attention tendency, an intriguing study was done in which participants were asked to count the number of times a basketball was passed among a group of people in a circle formation (Chabris & Simons 1999). The goal of participants who watched this was to correctly count the number of times the ball was passed. During the middle of the video, however, was a person explicitly dressed in an ape costume walking right through the middle of the people passing the ball around – even going so far as to gesture wildly to the camera while doing so. One would think that most, if not all, study participants viewing the episode would notice the ape strolling across the screen. However, because of the acute focus of participants trying to complete their given counting task, the majority of them failed to see the large ape at all – although most accurately guessed the number of passes made. If curious, this very popular clip, entitled "Selection Awareness Test," can be seen on YouTube.

Studies have also shown that people are more likely to make choices based on the need to avoid a negative experience rather than a positive experience, known as "prospect theory." Individuals also allocate more cognitive resources to negative information. In a study at the University of California, Berkeley, participants took longer to name a color that was associated with a negative personality trait relative to colors associated with positive personality traits (Pratto & John 1991). This difference in response times was attributed to participants devoting more attention to processing the trait itself when the associated personality trait was more negative than positive. Such research implies that individuals tend to recall negative traits more readily compared with positive traits. It also helps to explain why many individuals tend to recall past negative memories more easily than positive memories, leading to a tendency to underestimate past and future positive outcomes. Thus, to recall a person's memory, for better or for worse, a negative memory or experience will more likely be recalled than a positive one (arguably based on a survival bias innate in the human condition).

Studies have also demonstrated that people afford more respect to those who view and see things as negative rather than positive. A Stanford University study showed that people with a negative perspective on world affairs were viewed as more intelligent than those who took a more positive perspective on world affairs. In a related corollary, the English dictionary allocates 62 percent of all emotional words to those words with negative meanings or connotations (Gawdat 2017). As a senior fellow at the University of California, Berkeley's Greater Good Science Center stated, "The brain is like Velcro for negative experiences but Teflon for positive ones" (Hanson 2016).

Focusing more toward the positive impact of positive emotions, studies suggest that they have a strong effect on the mood levels of other individuals. In a paper from the University of Hawaii and Ohio University, researchers noted that participants were found to unconsciously feel the emotions of people around them – referred to as "emotional contagion." The authors argue that this phenomenon may occur because, as social animals, humans tend to mimic the movements and facial expressions of those within similar social groups (Hatfield, Cacioppo & Rapson 1993).

Positive emotions in the form of displaying a sense of humor have also been shown to increase attraction among individuals. In a study at DePaul University and Illinois State University, displaying humor when first meeting someone made participants like each other more (Treger, Sprecher & Erber 2013). Other research at Illinois State University and California State University, Los Angeles, demonstrated that participants sought humor in both their romantic partners as well as in their ideal friends (Sprecher & Regan 2002). Thus, the virtues of a sense of humor may have serious social value.

Persuasion and the personal touch

Research further suggests that similarities and shared belief systems increased likability. In a classic study, a "similarity-attraction effect" was found in the form of subjects liking their housemates more who shared similar attitudes on controversial topics, such as politics and sex (Newcomb 1956). In more recent research conducted at Washington University in St. Louis and the University of Virginia, Air Force recruits were found to view one another more favorably based on similar *negative* personality traits compared with shared positive traits (Tenney, Turkheimer & Oltmanns 2009).

Physically focusing on others was also found to have a demonstrable effect in terms of likability. The unobtrusive, light physical contact of others, such as lightly touching another's arm while talking, rationally should have no effect. But as individuals, the human touch fosters a positive perception. In a joint research study by the University of Mississippi and Rhodes College, food servers who briefly touched customers on the hand or shoulder when returning change from a paid bill received notably larger tips relative to instances where food servers made no physical contact (Crusco & Wetzel 1984). Similarly, in a French study involving young men standing on street corners tasked with talking to female strangers who were passing by, men who lightly touched the arms of women experienced double the success rate compared with those men who did not apply a light touch (Gueguen 2007). Thus, a light touch might serve as a Midas touch in terms of likability.

Subtly copying another individual's behavior, such as the counterparty's gestures, facial expressions, and language – referred to as mirroring – can also increase a sense of likability. As validated in a New York University study, researchers noted a "chameleon effect" in which the unconscious mimicking of paired participants' behavior facilitated a liking effect (Chartrand & Bargh 1999).

Sharing secrets was also found to increase likability. In a persuasion or negotiation context, parties must often decide whether to disclose certain confidential, non-public information, such as prices, processes, and profits. Such information would colloquially be referred to simply as personal or business secrets. However, research conducted at the State University of New York, Stony Brook; the California Graduate School of Family Psychology; the University of California, Santa Cruz; and Arizona State University showed that students who had asked to divulge information of a personal and private nature exhibited much closer feelings among paired groups than students who did not share such personal and private information (Aron, Melinat, Aron, Vallone & Bator 1997), Perhaps this is because sharing a secret is a form of revealing a vulnerability or weakness, which, in turn, signals trust, thus triggering reciprocity of such trust (linking to Cialdini's first principle of influence – reciprocity).

Sharing and spending more time with others – referred to as the "mere-exposure effect" – has also shown a correlation with increased likability among people who spend time together. In a study conducted at the University of Pittsburgh, students were asked to gauge preference levels of four women who posed as students in a university psychology course. Some of the four women attended several class lectures sitting in plain sight at the front of the lecture hall. The other women in the study did not attend any course lectures and thus were not seen by any students. Afterward, students in the course showed a stronger preference and likability toward those women who were actually seen in the class, even though each woman was viewed equally in terms of physical attraction overall (Moreland & Beach 1992). Thus, according to the study, seeing is not only believing, but also liking.

Case

Suppose a job applicant is about to enter into a highly stressful situation – a job interview. For this job applicant, landing a job with this organization would represent rarified air and a dream career come true.

Assume the interview process involves two stages. First, there is a document-screening stage, which requires the job applicant to submit a CV and cover letter detailing the job applicant's background, and why the job applicant believes she possesses the experience and skill sets necessary for the position. Based on the submitted documents, the organization then selects only a handful of applicants to enter the second stage: in-person interviews.

The prospect of facing a barrage of questions on-the-spot, and then being asked to respond immediately to such questions in real time, while being minutely critiqued on those answers can be daunting for almost anyone. For many students who are beginning their careers in the real world, it is an abrupt change from large lecture halls, university events, and late-night study sessions at the college library or cafe.

Suppose next that this same job applicant suddenly turns to the reader – seen by the job applicant as an apparent authority figure in the field of persuasion, influence, and negotiations – for sage counsel and actionable advice on the matter. The job applicant asks, "What specific psychological influences should be used to maximize the likelihood that the interviewer has a favorable opinion during and after the interview process?" In other words, what strategies of invisible influence and persuasion can and should be used – based on the actionable research in this chapter – to increase the chance that the interviewer will hire the student?

After all, hidden forces in the form of invisible influences can have verifiably visible effects.

Bibliography

Aron, A, Melinat, E, Aron, EN, Vallone, RD, & Bator, RJ 1997, 'The Experimental Generation of Interpersonal Closeness: A Procedure and Some Preliminary Findings', *Oxford University Libraries*. Available from: www.stafforini.com/txt/Aron%20et%20al%20-%20The%20experimental%20generation%20of%20interpersonal%20closeness.pdf. [5 January 2018].

Aronson, E, Willerman, B, & Floyd, J 1966, 'The Effect of Pratfall on Increasing Interpersonal Attractiveness', *Psychonomic Science*, vol. 4, no. 6, pp. 227–228. Available from: APA PsycNet. [15 December 2017].

Baumeister, RF, Bratslavsky, E, Finkenauer, C, & Vohs, KD 2001, 'Bad Is Stronger Than Good', *Review of General Psychology*, vol. 5, no. 4, pp. 323–370. Available from: http://dare.ubvu.vu.nl/bitstream/handle/1871/17432/Baumeister_Review%20of%20General%20Psychology_5 (4)_2001_u.pdf?sequence=2. [3 January 2018].

Bickman, L 1974, 'The Social Power of a Uniform', *Journal of Applied Social Psychology*, vol. 4, no. 1, pp. 47–61. Available from: Wiley Online Library. [2 January 2018].

Chabris, CF, & Simons, DJ 1999, 'Gorillas in Our Midst: Sustained Inattentional Blindness for Dynamic Events', *Perception*, vol. 28, pp. 1059–1074. Available from: www.chabris.com/Simons1999.pdf. [15 December 2017].

Chartrand, TL, & Bargh, JA 1999, 'The Chameleon Effect: The Perception-Behavior Link and Social Interaction', *Journal of Personality and Social Psychology*, vol. 76, no. 6, pp. 893–910. Available from: https://faculty.fuqua.duke.edu/~tlc10/bio/TLC_articles/1999/Chartrand_Bargh_1999.pdf. [15 December 2017].

Cialdini, RB 1993, *The Psychology Influence of Persuasion*, William Morrow and Company, New York.

Crusco, AH, & Wetzel, CG 1984, 'The Effects of Interpersonal Touch on Restaurant Tipping', *Personality and Social Psychology Bulletin*. Available from: http://journals.sagepub.com/doi/abs/10.1177/0146167284104003. [5 November 2017].

Fiske, S 2013, 'Integrating the Stereotype Content Model (Warmth and Competence) and the Osgood Semantic Differential (Evaluation, Potency, and Activity)', *European Journal of Social Psychology*. Available from: Woodrow Wilson School of Public & International Affairs. [15 November 2017].

Gawdat, M 2017, *Solve for Happy: Engineer Your Path to Joy*, Simon & Schuster, Inc., New York.

Gueguen, N 2007, 'Courtship Compliance: The Effect of Touch on Women's Behavior', *Social Influence*, vol. 2, no. 2, pp. 81–97. Available from: Taylor & Francis Group. [3 November 2017].

Hanson, R 2016, *Hardwiring Happiness: The New Brain Science of Contentment, Calm, and Confidence*, Harmony Books, New York.

Hatfield, E, Cacioppo, JT, & Rapson, RL 1993, 'Emotional Contagion', *Association for Psychological Science*, vol. 2, no. 3, pp. 96–100. Available from: Sage Journals. [11 November 2017].

McGinley, H, McGinley, P, & Nicholas, K 1978, 'Smiling, Body Position, and Interpersonal Attraction', *Bulletin of the Psychonomic Society*, vol. 12, no. 1, pp. 21–24. Available from: Link Springer. [13 November 2017].

Moreland, RL, & Beach, SR 1992, 'Exposure Effects in the Classroom: The Development of Affinity among Students', *Journal of Experimental Social Psychology*, vol. 28, no. 3, pp. 255–276. Available from: Elsevier. [5 November 2017].

Morris, M, Nadler, J, Kurtzberg, T, & Thompson, L 2002, 'Schmooze or Lose: Social Friction and Lubrication in E-mail Negotiations', *Group Dynamics: Theory, Research, and Practice*, vol. 6, no. 1, pp. 89–100. Available from: APA PsycNet. [5 January 2018].

Newcomb, TM 1956, 'The Prediction of Interpersonal Attraction', *American Psychologist*, vol. 11, no. 11, pp. 575–586. Available from: APA PsycNet. [21 December 2017].

Novotney, A 2014, 'The Psychology of Scarcity', *American Psychological Association*, vol. 45, no. 2, pp. 1–28. Available from: www.apa.org/monitor/2014/02/scarcity.aspx. [3 January 2018].

Pratto, F, & John, OP 1991, 'Automatic Vigilance: The Attention-Grabbing Power of Negative Social Information', *Journal of Personality and Social Psychology*, vol. 61, no. 3, pp. 380–391. Available from: http://pdfs.semanticscholar.org/1b21/ac00ee5749b94444183b2729397b762f093d.pdf. [17 December 2017].

Righi, S, Gronchi, G, Marzi, T, Mohamed, R, & Viggiano, MP 2015, 'You Are That Smiling Guy I Met at the Party! Socially Positive Signals Foster Memory for Identities and Contexts', *Acta Psychologica*, vol. 159, pp. 1–7. Available from: Elsevier. [22 December 2017].

Robinson, DT, & Smith-Lovin, L 1992, 'Selective Interaction as a Strategy for Identity Maintenance: An Affect Control Model', *Social Psychology Quarterly*, vol. 55, no. 1, pp. 12–28. Available from: Jstor. [5 November 2017].

Skowronski, JJ, Carlston, DE, Mae, L, & Crawford, MT 1998, 'Spontaneous Trait Transference: Communicators Taken on the Qualities They Describe in Others', *Journal of Personality and Social Psychology*, vol. 74, no. 4, pp. 837–848. Available from: NCBI. [3 November 2017].

Sprecher, S, & Regan, PC 2002, 'Liking Some Things (in Some People) More Than Others: Partner Preferences in Romantic Relationships and Friendships', *Journal of Social and Personal Relationships*, vol. 19, no. 4. Available from: Sage Journals. [11 November 2017].

Strohmetz, DB, Rind, B, Fisher, R, & Lynn, M 2002, 'Sweetening the Till: The Use of Candy to Increase Restaurant Tipping', *Journal of Applied Social Psychology*, vol. 32, no. 2, pp. 300–309. Available from: Wiley Online Library. [7 November 2017].

Tamir, DI, & Mitchell, JP 2012, 'Disclosing Information about the Self Is Intrinsically Rewarding', *PNAS*, vol. 109, no. 21. Available from: www.pnas.org/content/109/21/8038.full. [5 January 2018].

Tenney, ER, Turkheimer, E, & Oltmanns, TF 2009, 'Being Liked Is More Than Having a Good Personality: The Role of Matching', *Journal of Research in Personality*, vol. 43, no. 4, pp. 579–585. Available from: NCBI. [5 January 2018].

Treger, S, Sprecher, S, & Erber, R 2013, 'Laughing and Liking: Exploring the Interpersonal Effects of Humor Use in Initial Social Interactions', *European Journal of Social Psychology*, vol. 43, no. 6, pp. 532–543. Available from: Wiley Online Library. [7 November 2017].

2 Judgments
Surprising shortcuts toward judgments

Heuristics (mental shortcuts)

Persuasion and decision-making are fundamentally interlinked. To demonstrate this, here is a simple thought experiment: Assume a voter must decide between two political candidates for an upcoming election. Should the voter choose Candidate A or Candidate B?

A voter's decision is often based on who the voter finds more persuasive in terms of the issues that matter most to the voter in question. However, when viewing the profiles of both candidates, the typical voter is often overwhelmed with statistics, figures, and narratives offered by newspapers, blogs, political pundits, debates, and other resources. The political opinions of which candidate to vote for are also often bombarded upon potential voters – both solicited and unsolicited – from family, friends, acquaintances, and colleagues, among others.

If the voter was fully rational, all the available information would in theory be considered for analysis. In such Rationalist process, the voter (and any other similarly situated decision-maker) would constantly calibrate all the available information from now until election day, weighing all such information to come to a final analysis. This final analysis would then be directly reflected in the voting ballot – for one candidate over another – on election day.

In theory, in a perfect world, this rational choice scenario sounds exactly like how voters "ought" to act. But in practice, does it always accurately conform to how voters "actually" act in reality? Do theory and practice clash or conform? This is a thematic question within this chapter and this book.

Choosing between two candidates may seem relatively straightforward for certain individuals. So take another example that also affects many people worldwide: the 2008 subprime mortgage crisis.

Many people are aware of those who were directly impacted by, or may have been directly impacted herself or himself by the 2008 subprime financial crisis. From this, an analysis can be made in terms of what the typical mortgage borrower ought in theory to have done (by Rationalists under rational choice theory) versus what the mortgage borrower actually likely did in the real world (by Behavioralists in an applied setting where theory confronts practice) in the years surrounding the 2008 subprime crisis.

First, the mortgage borrower ought to have scrupulously and diligently conducted research on what properties to buy relative to other properties based on rational economic decision-making using a cost-benefit analysis. Once a decision was made, it was time to contractually commit to a particular property. Here, the individual would then have read over dozens, if not hundreds, of pages of dense, dry, and highly technical legalese relating to the property purchase, including legal terminology relating to the prime or subprime mortgage loan documents. For the average layperson, many of the embedded legal terms would be unfamiliar and downright daunting. In a fully rational world consistent with rational behavior, the borrower ought to have dutifully and diligently searched for the specific meaning and interpretation of each material unknown term for each possible contextual interpretation for the jurisdiction in question. On the economic side, above and beyond the legal considerations, the economic ramifications of interest-only payments, amortization, and adjustable rate mortgages (ARMs) versus fixed-rate mortgages (FRMs), using multiple scenario analyses (accounting for such things as interest rate fluctuations and exogenous economic shocks) would also in theory have all been duly considered and incorporated into the borrower's cost-benefit analysis. This would have been done in many cases alongside holding a full-time job, taking care of family duties, as well as meeting other professional and social obligations.

But does such rational behavior accurately reflect what actually occurred during the 2008 subprime crisis?

Often when individuals encounter an overload of information, mental shortcuts called "heuristics" are used by the brain in an effort to make a decision. Following is a more formalized definition for the term "heuristic":

> A heuristic is a rule of thumb, strategy, trick, simplification, or any other kind of device which drastically limits the search for solutions in large problem spaces. Heuristics do not guarantee optimal solutions.
> Feigenbaum & Feldman 1963, p. 61

Now consider how voters, and more broadly, people in general—from businesspersons and beauticians to bankers and bureaucrats—make decisions. Do such individuals constantly and consistently make decisions "rationally," considering all available information at all times to render a finely calibrated cost-benefit analysis decision? And in more instances than not, in the real world, would this rational process actually be the one that governs the day for all people at all times – or are heuristics at times used as cognitive shortcuts in decision-making processes?

This then leads to the concept of rational behavior linked to rational choice theory (RCT). But first, what does rationality mean? Of course, like with much of academic terminology, the term "rationality" has many definitions based on varying interpretations. But certain hallmark traits of rationality include maximizing utility, preferences under uncertainty, and transitivity (Blume & Easley 2007).

In the case of preferences, consistency is a key element. For example, rationality does not speak to an individual preferring soup over salads. But it may be counter to rationality to prefer soup over salad in one context, but salad over soup in another context (Sen 1969). This links to the issue of transitivity underlying rational behavior. At the basic level, transitivity states that if A is preferred over B, and B is preferred over C, then A must be preferred over C. This follows the logical construct of A > B > C; therefore A > C.

But do individuals always hold true to transitivity?

In many cases, the evidence suggests yes. But in certain exceptional cases, the evidence suggests no.

This is because individuals are often overwhelmed with information. As a result, individuals sometimes seek mental shortcuts as a means to make decisions under time constraints. Under the circumstances of everyday lives, in the current 24/7 world of constant connectivity, most, if not all, individuals are subject to some level of time constraint.

Heuristics can include associations and priming, judgments, substitution, cognitive bases, stories and causes, and emotions.

Priming

Priming is an unconscious behavior of the human brain that is linked with identification of objects, numbers, and words (Hoey 2005). Priming activates particular associations or linkages prior to executing a particular task. For example, a person who is told or reads the word "red" may then recognize the word "apple" faster. This is because of the association an individual often makes between "red" and "apple" in one's memory based on the past. As such, priming an individual before a particular task can assert a certain hidden force upon that individual's selection or decision-making processes.

If individuals were truly rational in the traditional sense, then priming should not have any effect. After all, what occurs before a particular decision should not in theory directly affect subsequent decision-making processes or decision-making outcomes since such choices should be viewed independently. To illustrate the point, think of the perfect rational choice theorist – a computer (or computing device). A (perfectly rational) computer, when tasked to make a particular decision, would not be adversely or positively affected or influenced by the mere contextual exposure to a particular word, symbol, act, or number. But for many humans, this type of behavior exists, and as such, hidden forces like priming can influence rational choice (Berger 2017).

A classic study on priming involved individuals exposed to words associated with stereotypes of the elderly (Bargh, Chen & Burrows 1996). Study participants who were exposed to words like "retirement" were found to walk more slowly than those who were shown words not typically associated with the elderly. What is notable about this elderly-slow study is not only that participants were found to observe certain traits in others when primed with associated words, but also that participants were more likely to physically act in a way that was consistent with such word association.

Similarly, another study suggested that those primed with a trigger-trait word, such as "stubborn," were more likely to find this same trait when observing others. Even more, when primed with the concept of an academic or professor prior to taking a general knowledge test, participants performed better. This is the same case for those primed with pictures of Rodin's *The Thinking Man*, which boosted academic performance (Cialdini 2016). Conversely, when primed with (fashion) supermodel associations, test takers performed more poorly.

The reader may also be curious as to the short- or long-term effect of priming. A paper focusing on national and political identity involving Israeli participants centered on this question (Hassin, Ferguson, Shidlovski & Gross 2007). As many are aware, Israeli politics often harbor deep divides on political issues, such as border security, the Palestinian state, and relations with Israel's neighbor countries. But will seeing the image of an Israeli flag – even for less a second – prime participants to be reminded of the common national identity of the Israeli state, underlying such deep political divides?

In the study, groups were shown 60 images. Each image was shown for one-sixtieth of a second (literally, a split second). In this super-short period, the mind does not have time to consciously recognize the split-second visual image shown to the participant. For one group, the split-second image shown was of the Israeli flag. For another group, the split-second image shown was a scattered image of the Israeli flag (scattered to such an extent that participants would be unable to recognize an Israeli flag, even with more time given). The study found that the answer to the original question was yes. Those who were shown the Israeli flag image tended to vote relatively more moderately (since a singular flag reflected a singular and thus more unified country). In contrast, those who were shown the image of a scattered Israeli flag tended to vote less moderately (voting for left- and right-of-center political parties and platforms). Thus, priming had an effect on furthering national and political identity. Not only did the study's data find such correlation, but also such correlation existed for several months afterward, specifically within the months leading up to an election and the election itself (Hassin, Ferguson, Shidlovski & Gross 2007). The takeaway here is that not only can priming promote associations, but also that such associations can have longer than a short-term effect.

Priming also is present for those who enjoy fine dining in French restaurants. Several French researchers found that restaurant patrons gave different levels of tips based on a one-sentence quote written on the restaurant bill (Lynn 2015). The study involved three cases: (1) patrons whose bill had an altruistic quote: "A good turn never goes amiss"; (2) patrons whose bill had a neutral quote: "He who writes reads twice"; and (3) patrons whose bill did not have any phrase written on it. Ensuring in the study that all patrons took note of the writings, the French study revealed that those patrons left with the altruistic quote gave relatively more in tips (above and beyond the standard 12 percent automatic add-on). Tipping was also influenced by the color red and physical distance between the food server and restaurant patron.

What about priming's effects not involving visible wording, numbers, or images, specifically something like music? Think of all the places where music is played either at the forefront (concerts) or in the background (cafes, department stores). Can the invisible and seemingly innocuous playing of music – such as the playing of subtle background music – represent a hidden force, and thus, influence the decision-making of individuals?

The short answer is yes. Not only was background music found to affect decision-making, but also it was shown to have the power to increase altruism (Gueguen & Jacob 2012). In today's world, this could certainly be useful. After all, altruism involving helping others could have profound effects on donations to charities, and helping those in need in a myriad of prosocial endeavors. Altruism is also the antidote to aggression, suppression, selfishness, and invidious discrimination, which can represent a dark side of hidden forces within persuasion, influence, and negotiation contexts.

Evidence of how music affects individuals is seen in a study by Australian psychologist Tobias Greitemeyer, which showed that playing music with "prosocial" lyrics and themes ("Help," "Heal the World," "We Are The World") primed people to both think and act in ways that were associated with prosocial behavior, including giving charitable contributions to nonprofit organizations (Greitemeyer 2009).

Judgments

Hidden heuristics, a form of hidden forces, are often used involving judgments under uncertainty – perceived risks and benefits, known-unknown variables, and derivative forms of information asymmetry. Judgments in such contexts are often based on cognitive processes that may link to heuristics. Here, the cognitive process is attempting to employ a practical solution to solve an immediate cognitive problem.

One aspect of rational behavior is the attempted accurate assignment of probabilistic outcomes (reasoning) to uncertain situations. Here, the heuristics of *representativeness, base-rates, availability, framing,* and *anchoring* are used. These are used to predict probabilities and values. These heuristics relating to judgment under uncertainty are often effective, but can lead to predictable and systematic errors (Tversky & Kahneman 1974). Often, individuals are unaware of such downsides. Given this, such shortcuts can often be predictably and unknowingly wrong.

Representativeness

The *representativeness heuristic* occurs when an object or event A resembles some other object or event B, in which an individual infers and implies similarity in class or category between A and B, although not fully considering the probability of event B occurring, which is illustrated later with an example (Bar-Hillel 1984).

This is separate from the *base-rate heuristic*, which is a mental shortcut that also helps make decisions based on probability. For example, if a driver hears a vehicle honking on the highway, the driver would probably guess it is a car (not truck or other vehicle type) that is honking because there are generally more cars than trucks on the road overall. The base-rate heuristic does have its downsides. For example, when describing individuals from different regions around the world, the base-rate heuristic may not capture a comprehensive picture of such individuals, such as height and weight of individuals in every region.

An example of representativeness is showing in the following:

> Bob is very good with numbers and likes money. He also is very materialistic. Bob often engages in constant conspicuous consumption, including buying fancy sports cars and wearing flashy clothing.
> Bob is most likely:
>
> A.   An investment banker
> B.   A government worker

Many individuals may choose A that Bob is most likely an investment banker by occupation, as a result of the representativeness heuristic. Here, the characteristics of engaging in conspicuous consumption, buying fancy cars, and wearing trendy clothing may be more associated with the fast and furious lifestyle of a banker, particularly bearing the media's images in the pejorative of bankers during the wake of the 2008 subprime mortgage crisis. However, the likelihood (base-rate) of Bob being a government worker is relatively higher since, first, there are many more government workers overall in a country relative to investment bankers, and second, that investment banking represents a highly specialized subset within the broader banking sector.

Availability

The *availability heuristic* is a mental shortcut that can be used in persuasion and decision-making based on the ability to relate the current situation to one that comes easiest to mind. The ease with which the mind can recall a particular event can affect the individual's estimates of the predicted future probability of such event. Even more, a vivid instance or piece of information is more easily recalled and thus more convincing. In other words, the mind tries to think of easy-to-recall examples that are similar enough (but not exactly or perfectly similar) to the current situation at hand when estimating the probability of an event occurring or not.

Applying the availability heuristic to practice is the following query: What percentage of all crimes were violent crimes in the United States in 2011? Many people are likely to guess a high percentage because of the vast media attention given to violent crimes, such as murder, rape, robbery, and assault. Yet FBI statistics show that violent crimes made up less than 12 percent of all crimes (FBI Crime Statistics 2012). Another example of the availability heuristic involves people being asked whether it was more dangerous to drive by car or fly by plane (Hint: the answer is by car) (Dimara, Dragicevic & Bezerianos 2014).

Framing

The *framing heuristic* is another mental shortcut and hidden force in which the selection among given choices may be affected by the way in which such choices are presented (framed) as gains (benefits) or losses (risks). This is despite the fact that both are numerically equivalent. The framing heuristic is thus an extremely subtle yet significant hidden force in persuasion.

As examples, given a disease outbreak scenario, 75 percent of subjects chose the risk-averse option when the problem was framed as a gain (choice A below framed as saving lives) even though both options had identical probability outcomes – for example, choices: (A) 200 lives saved; or (B) one-third chance of 600 lives saved and two-thirds chance of no lives saved (Tversky & Kahneman 1974). In contrast, 78 percent of subjects chose to take action (risk-taking option) when the choice was framed in terms of losses (choice A below framed as losses) even though both options had identical probability outcomes (choices: (A) 400 lives lost, or (B) one-third chance of no lives lost and two-thirds chance of 600 lives lost). The takeaway here is that a framing effect was evident. As such, the way the question was framed led to dramatically different actions and outcomes by individuals—to take action over inaction. However, as rational choice actors, the framing effect should in theory have little or no effect whatsoever.

Anchoring

The *anchoring heuristic* is another mental shortcut and hidden force in which the mere exposure to arbitrary numbers or biased information (the anchor) can affect people's prediction of values. This is the case even when individuals involved in the study were explicitly told that the arbitrary numbers and information were completely unrelated.

As an example, perhaps one of the gravest existential threats facing human-kind today is the threat of nuclear war. When individuals were exposed to an arbitrary number of 1 percent (anchor), and then subsequently asked to predict the probability of nuclear war, those exposed to the 1 percent anchor gave lower estimates than people not exposed to a low anchor. However, people exposed to a 99 percent anchor gave higher estimates for the likeli-hood of nuclear war compared with those not exposed to any anchor or a lower anchor. Since it is important to accurately determine such risk and threat level, in an idyllic world, leaders who are placed in such situations hopefully will not succumb as easily to the possible persuasive and hidden effects of anchors prior to making nuclear security decisions.

The anchoring heuristic is, of course, not just confined to estimates of nuclear war. Studies demonstrate that the anchoring effect has influence on everyday negotiations in the form of first offers – even aggressive first offers – whereby such first offers served as anchors that correlated with sub-sequent, final, and agreed-upon negotiated outcomes (Galinsky & Muss-weiler 2001). As every reader of this book has entered into one form of negotiation or another – formal or informal, personal or professional – the influence of the framing effect is significant in both scale and scope.

Case

Imagine having to give a talk in front of a large audience. It is crucial that the audience have a positive view of the session. This includes the audience's perception of the speaker. Before going onstage, an assistant asks, "Would you (the speaker) prefer a cold or hot drink to take with you onstage?"

Should holding a cold or hot drink have any influence on the way that the speaker is perceived by the audience (in-person and/or online)?

The judging of a person's character is critical. People do it constantly, albeit consciously or unconsciously. Often the judging of another's character can come at critical times in one's career arc. Examples include giving a talk in front of a large audience (such as in this scenario), a job interview in front of interviewers, evaluations for a promotion by one's supervisors, or student evaluations of a particular professor.

One not uncommon metric in terms of determining character is generosity or warmth. Such characteristics may be linked by some with greater cooperation, which is important when working or functioning in group settings. Given this, here is the question: What could be an effective, efficient, and ethical priming tool that would elicit a sense of warmth and compassion from the audience?

Smiling is often viewed as a cooperation signal. As such, smiling may help with being viewed as generous or warm. Colors worn also have shown to have an influential effect. But perhaps more innocuously, what about holding a hot drink compared with holding a cold, iced drink?

In today's coffee culture, it is fairly common to see individuals quickly dashing from one meeting to the next with a cup of coffee, tea, or other drink in hand. It turns out that – at least from a persuasion and priming context – the seemingly small matter of the temperature of such drink can make a big difference.

A seminal study conducted at Yale University revealed that people viewed others as more generous and caring if such other individuals were holding hot drinks (rather than cold drinks). In another study, participants were found to give more after holding a warm drink rather than a cold drink (assessing others as significantly "warmer"). Conversely, participants were found to take more after holding a cold drink rather than a warm drink. From a policy perspective, such findings could also have tangible spillover effects in terms of priming others to engage in prosocial behavior that would foster greater cooperation.

So next time, when given the seemingly innocuous choice of a holding a hot drink or a cold drink, choose the hot drink. Doing so will foster a greater sense of generosity and warmth.

Bibliography

Bargh, JA, Chen, M, & Burrows, L 1996, 'Automaticity of Social Behavior: Direct Effects of Trait Construct and Stereotype Activation on Action', *Journal of Personality and Social Psychology*, vol. 71, no. 2, pp. 230–244. Available from: http://citeseerx.ist.psu.edu/viewdoc/download?doi=10.1.1.333.7523&rep=rep1& type=pdf. [3 January 2018].

Bar-Hillel, M 1984, 'Representativeness and Fallacies of Probability Judgment', *Acta Psychologica*, vol. 55, no. 2, pp. 91–107. Available from: Elsevier. [5 January 2018].

Berger, J 2017, *Invisible Influence: The Hidden Forces That Shape Behavior*, Simon & Schuster, Inc., New York.

Blume, LE, & Easley, D 2007, 'Rationality', *The Santa Fe Institute*. Available from: http://tuvalu.santafe.edu/~leb/rat03.pdf. [28 October 2017].

Cialdini, R 2016, *Pre-Suasion: A Revolutionary Way to Influence and Persuade*, Simon & Schuster, Inc., New York.

Dimara, E, Dragicevic, P, & Bezerianos, A 2014, *Accounting for Availability Biases in Information Visualization*. Available from: https://arxiv.org/pdf/1610.02857. pdf. [3 January 2018].

Federal Bureau of Investigation 2012, *National Press Releases*. Available from: https://archives.fbi.gov/archives/news/pressrel/press-releases/fbi-releases-2011-crime-statistics. [5 November 2017].

Feigenbaum, EA, & Feldman, J 1963, *Computers and Thought*, McGraw-Hill Inc., New York.

Galinsky, AD, & Mussweiler, T 2001, 'First Offers as Anchors: The Role of Perspective-Taking and Negotiator Focus', *Journal of Personality and Social Psychology*, vol. 81, no. 4, pp. 657–669. Available from: www.communicationcache.com/uploads/1/0/8/8/10887248/first_offers_as_anchors-_the_role_of_perspective-taking_and_negotiator_focus.pdf. [15 November 2017].

Greitemeyer, T 2009, 'Effects of Songs with Prosocial Lyrics on Prosocial Behavior: Further Evidence and a Mediating Mechanism', *Personality and Social Psychology Bulletin*, vol. 35, no. 11. Available from: Sage Journals. [12 October 2017].

Gueguen, N, & Jacob, C 2012, 'Congruency between Instrumental Background Music and Behavior on a Website', *Psychology of Music*, vol. 42, no. 1. Available from: Sage Journals. [17 October 2017].

Hassin, RR, Ferguson, MJ, Shidlovski, D, & Gross, T 2007, 'Subliminal Exposure to National Flags Affects Political Thought and Behavior', *PNAS*, vol. 104, no. 50, pp. 19757–19761. Available from: www.pnas.org/content/104/50/19757.full. [5 November 2017].

Hoey, M 2005, *Lexical Priming: A New Theory of Words and Language*, Routledge, New York.

Lynn, M 2015, 'Service Gratuities and Tipping: A Motivational Framework', *The Scholarly Commons*. Available from: http://scholarship.sha.cornell.edu/cgi/viewcontent.cgi?article=1588&context=articles. [7 November 2017].

Plous, S 1989, 'Thinking the Unthinkable: The Effects of Anchoring on Likelihood Estimates of Nuclear War', *Journal of Applied Social Psychology*, vol. 19, no. 1, pp. 67–91. Available from: Wiley Online Library. [8 November 2017].

Sen, A 1969, 'Quasi-Transitivity, Rational Choice and Collective Decisions', *The Review of Economic Studies*, vol. 36, no. 3, pp. 381–393. Available from: Jstor. [5 December 2017].

Tversky, A, & Kahneman, D 1974, 'Judgment under Uncertainty: Heuristics and Biases', *Science*, vol. 185, no. 4157, pp. 1124–1131. Available from: Jstor. [7 December 2017].

3 Biases
The blind side of hidden biases

Cognitive illusions

Non-rational tendencies are sometimes colloquially referred to as biases (a form of cognitive illusion). In persuasion, perception can lead to reality. This is, in part, because persuasion is often a perception game, which is evidenced by a series of studies and scientific research.

In a study by Kahneman, Knetsch & Thaler (1991), individuals tended to place a higher value on those goods that they owned themselves, as opposed to an exact same good owned by others, in what is known as the endowment effect (also referred to as divestiture aversion). In an experiment, researchers discovered that participants' *perception* of value changed based on who owned a particular item, counter to rational choice theory whereby who owns a particular good should generally not influence pricing. In another experiment, participants were given either a lottery ticket (purchased for $2) or $2 in cash. Sometime later, those subjects given the lottery ticket were given the opportunity to trade the lottery ticket for $2, and vice versa (Kahneman, Knetsch & Thaler 1991). Under rational choice theory, many should have swapped since both have identical monetary values. But in an interesting twist, very few people chose to swap their originally given item.

In a similar but separate study, people were given a ticket for a college sports event (the NCAA Final Four basketball tournament), and were then asked to determine a hypothetical selling price for the ticket (known as a Willingness To Accept, or WTA). Although some premium may be expected to offset costs associated with the transaction, it turned out that the average selling price was a stunning 14 times higher than the ticket's purchase price (known as the Willingness To Pay, or WTP), primarily driven by a psychological phenomenon known as ownership bias (Carmon & Ariely 2000). In both experiments, if individuals were fully rational, then the fact that the owner is selling a good should not influence the perceived value of that good. Nor should mere ownership command such an exorbitant selling price premium. But such studies and others surprisingly suggest owning an item drives up its perceived value, sometimes significantly. As owners, many people find ways to justify their particular product as unique and special in some way, no matter how subjective, in an attempt to create and then justify an extremely elevated price.

Going beyond self-ownership and value perception to perception of value based on who made such proposal, evidence also suggests individuals tend to diminish the value of a particular proposal based on who is making such proposal. For example, in a negotiation context, individuals were found to devalue the merits of an offered proposal without considering its benefits, merely because such offer came from the negotiation counterparty (the other side). This is referred to as reactive devaluation. In a related study, researchers found that when former US President Ronald Reagan submitted an idea to his constituents, the American people, 90 percent of respondents had a favorable or neutral view of the idea. However, when this very same idea was proposed by Mikhail Gorbachev (former leader of the USSR), only 44 percent of Americans held a favorable or neutral view (Ross & Stillinger 1991). In a similar study, Israeli-Jews evaluated an Israeli-authored peace plan less favorably when it was attributed to a Palestinian author or group than when it was attributed to their own government (Maoz, Ward, Katz & Ross 2002). Here, the messenger truly becomes the message.

Individuals were also found to be overconfident (above and beyond average confidence levels) of their own individual abilities. This is known as the overconfidence effect, which leads not just to overconfidence, but also to overestimation, and overplacement of one's own abilities and outcomes. One explanation for this psychological phenomenon is that wishful (positive) thinking can often overly encourage individuals to believe that events will turn out positively in their favor. Such self-esteem can then lead many individuals to overrate the quality and accuracy of one's judgments, and, in turn, undervalue the likelihood for mistakes.

In related findings, on average, negotiators believed they had more than a 60 percent chance of winning their negotiation. While this may not seem overly optimistic, consider that only 50 percent of all parties typically win in a negotiation with two parties involved. So the 10 percent gap (or premium) above and beyond 50 percent arguably signals overconfidence by parties (Lim 1997). Likewise, financial investors were found to overestimate the quality of information they had, as well as their ability to analyze, interpret, and take market action based on the financial information they had. Such overconfidence effect gave individuals the illusion of controlling financial market developments, while also arguably distorting their risk assessment to a low level, leading such investors to take much greater risk (Lim 1997). As takeaways, these types of findings should have served as shots across the bow for the dot-com boom-and-bust scenario of the early 2000s as well as the 2008 global subprime crisis.

Individuals also tended to believe that they were fairly objective in their own perception and analysis of people and situations, relative to others, when it turned out this was not the case. This cognitive illusion is referred to as naive realism (sometimes called direct realism). It is a psychological phenomenon in persuasion whereby individuals believe that they see the world objectively while others do not, and that others who do see the world differently are simply uninformed, irrational, or biased. Ironically, however, it is the individual in question who in fact may be the biased one. The expression, "My truth should be your truth" encapsulates this concept of naive realism.

In a related study involving two soccer team supporters from opposite competing teams, each soccer team supporter side reacted very differently when viewing the exact same game. This occurred because each side perceived the game quite differently. Although reacting differently, both sides believed that they were watching the game objectively, and that it was the other side's perception (not their own) that was distorted and biased (Hastorf & Cantril 1954). In another study, participants were told to tap a particular chosen rhythm of a well-known song, while listener-participants were asked to try to identify the song that was being tapped to them. Prior to beginning the tapping, the music tappers estimated that their chosen song would be guessed accurately about 50 percent of the time. However, in reality, the listeners were only able to identify the song approximately 2.5 percent of the time, representing a remarkable overconfidence gap (Heath & Heath 2006)

Cognitive illusions, counter to rational behavior, within individuals also surfaced in cases where multiple conditions were assumed to be more likely to be true than a single one (even though the occurrence of multiple, simultaneous conditions was statistically less likely than the occurrence of a single event by itself). This cognitive trap is referred to as conjunction fallacy (also colloquially known as The Linda Problem).

As an example of the conjunction fallacy, here is a short background profile of Linda:

Linda is 31 years old, single, outspoken, and very bright. She majored in philosophy in university. As a student, she was deeply concerned with issues of social justice and discrimination. Linda also participated in political and anti-nuclear proliferation demonstrations. Which is more likely to be true about Linda?

A. Linda is a bank teller
B. Linda is a bank teller and is active in the feminist movement

Now read the following background profile of a different person, Jean:

> Jean went to a convenience store and bought tofu, avocado, eggplant, broccoli, and frozen meatless lasagna to cook for dinner. Which of the following statements is more likely to be true about Jean?
>
> A.   Jean is a woman
> B.   Jean is a woman and a vegetarian

With both questions, most participants in a related study believed that B (the second option) was more likely to be true. In the bank teller question, about 85 percent chose B. This is despite the fact that it is less likely that Linda would be both a bank teller and active in the feminist movement (since it is more unlikely to have two traits compared with having just a single trait). In the second food purchase example, many participants chose B (the second option), deciding that it was more likely that Jean was both a woman and vegetarian rather than only being a woman. However, the cognitive trap here, as before, is that it cannot be assumed that Jean is a vegetarian just because Jean bought vegetables and meatless lasagna for one particular occasion (Siades, Osherson, Bonini & Viale 2002).

Interesting patterns also appeared in people's spending patterns. Individuals were found to make errors in mental accounting, known as the denomination effect. Given an equivalent sum of money, the likelihood of spending a single large denomination (a single $20 bill, equaling $20) was lower than when the same amount was in many small denominations (twenty $1 bills, equaling $20). In a related study, participants were given one dollar in two different forms: 25 cents or a single $1 bill. The participants were then given the option of buying candy with this money or saving it. Those who were given 25 cents spent their money more often than those participants who were given a single $1 bill (Raghubir & Sriivastava 2009). Individuals also opted to use coins rather than paper bills when using vending machines to buy candy or drinks.

On a similar topic of calculations, individuals were often found to clash with rational behavior when it came to investment decisions. In a securities trading context, investors demonstrated a tendency to sell their losing investments quickly while also demonstrating a tendency to hold winning investments in a form of "selling losers, and keeping winners." This is more formally known as the disposition effect.

As an applied example of the disposition effect, read and answer the following questions:

Which one of the following two options should be chosen?

A. 50 percent chance of gaining $1,000; or
B. 100 percent chance of gaining $500

With $2,000 in hand (in a securities trading context), should A or B be chosen?

A. 50 percent chance of losing $1,000; or
B. 100 percent chance of losing $500

With the initial question, participants generally chose B. This is because when choices are framed as a gain, participants were found to be more risk-averse, thus being persuaded by the relatively safer, more secure option B, 100 percent chance of gaining $500 (in a form of "don't lose what you already have"). In the next question, however, the majority of participants chose A, 50 percent chance of losing $1,000. When framed as a loss, participants tended to be risk-seeking in an effort to "get out of the hole," leading participants to focus on the 50 percent chance of not losing money (Weber & Camerer 1998). In sum, individuals disliked losing money more than they liked gaining money.

Individual decision-making was also found to be skewed (again, counter to rational decision-making theory) when it came to estimating the likelihood of future events or outcomes, referred to as the Law of Large Numbers (LLN) (or more colloquially, the hot hands fallacy or gambler's fallacy). This phenomenon is reflected in the mistaken (seemingly irrational) belief that if an event occurs more frequently than normal during a given time period, this will then lead to an event occurring more frequently in the future (or vice versa relating to less frequent events occurring).

To demonstrate LLN, the following question is given:

Which of the following would be more true if a basketball player who averages 50 percent at the free throw line has successfully just made five consecutive free throws?

A. A 50 percent likelihood still exists of making the next free throw, despite having made five consecutive free throws
B. A greater than 50 percent likelihood of making the free throw exists since the player is clearly in a "hot streak" and/or in "a zone"

The answer is A, if individuals were truly rational. A rough corollary would be the flipping of a coin. A coin can land on either heads or tails. Given statistical probability (based on infinite iterations), there is a 50 percent likelihood that the coin will land on heads (or tails) – even if the coin landed on heads five, 50, or 100 consecutive times. This is because, linked to LLN, is a reversion to the mean effect, in which event outcomes will revert back to the expected mean level over the course of increasing iterations (such as coin flips or free throws made). But as Behavioralists will point out, the story-telling side of humans as social animals can have a demonstrable spillover effect into media narratives and decision-making that is both potentially pervasive and persuasive.

People's perceptions were also found to be influenced by the timing of an event. Specifically, studies suggest that individual judgment is based on feelings during the peak and end of an experience. This is referred to as the peak-end rule, as typified in Shakespeare's maxim, "All's well that ends well." In studies, participants were found to intuitively end their social interactions on a positive note to build positive experiences and strengthen interpersonal connections (Kahneman, Fredrickson, Schreiber & Redelmeier 1993; Albert & Kessler 1978). Similarly, a majority of test subjects chose to repeat one trial over another trial (that was an objectively more painful trial), in which pain in the original trial was gradually reduced toward the end, and thus was perceived by many participants as less painful overall (Schneider, Stone & Broderick 2011).

Timing also influenced perception in terms of events occurring prior to a given event. Specifically, individuals demonstrated a tendency to wrongly (irrationally) assume causality between two sequential events in a form of "Event Y followed event X; therefore, event X must have caused event Y." This is referred to as illusory correlation (in Latin, as *post hoc ergo procter hoc*, or more colloquially, "correlation is causation"). For example, a baseball player may attribute a particular ritual or lucky bat as the reason for hitting more home runs in a game. Here, one event is followed (correlated) by the other, with the baseball player directly attributing a causal connection between the two events. Similarly, people suffering from migraine headaches often blame particular foods, sounds, or even atmospheric changes (rainy weather) as sources of their migraine attacks (Hoffman & Recober 2013). In another example, an old woman, for instance, may believe that sharks are extremely dangerous. When she reads about a swimmer being injured in the news, given this schema (mental categorization), she then may automatically assume it was a shark that attacked someone, although it instead could have been due to any reason, such as being hit by a surfboard, inability to swim, or being stung by a jellyfish (Hamilton & Gifford 1976).

Repetition and rhyming were also found to impact perception, and thus, lead to biased decision-making. Related research suggests that greater exposure leads to greater familiarity to something or someone, which, in turn, leads to greater liking or preference of that particular thing or person. This psychological bias is referred to as the mere exposure effect (MEE) (or more colloquially, the familiarity principle), and is encapsulated in the expression, "familiarity breeds likability." The MEE refers to increased liking because of repeated exposure, which exists in a wide variety of stimuli (visual, auditory, olfactory), in a broad array of contexts (laboratory, field, commercials) (Zajonic 1968). As such, MEEs can have numerous real-world ramifications, including with repetitive ads, voting behavior, and more generally, people who surround us every day who repeat certain statements or stories.

Rhyming has also, interestingly enough, been correlated with perceived truthfulness by individuals. Such cognitive bias in which phrases and arguments that rhyme are believed to be more true than those that do not rhyme is known as the "rhyme and reason effect." Examples include "health is wealth" and "If the glove don't fit, then you must acquit." In a study related to the accuracy of aphorisms as descriptions of human behavior, rhyming aphorisms ("What sobriety conceals, alcohol reveals") were perceived to be more accurate than those aphorisms that did not rhyme ("What sobriety conceals, alcohol unmasks") (McGlone & Tofighbakhsh 2000).

Pictures also impact perception leading to biased behavior as hidden forces. Research findings suggest that pictures and images are more likely to be remembered than words. This is referred to as the picture superiority effect, as exemplified in the maxim, "A picture is worth a thousand words." In a published study, items were more accurately recalled in recognition memory tasks when studied as visual pictures than words. This was the case even when the actual test phrase was conducted in a word-based presentation (Defeyter, Russo & McPartlin 2009). Moreover, graphic pictures in anti-tobacco messages had a vastly larger impact in portraying the health threat of smoking compared with worded messages without pictures, as exemplified by a cigarette pack with a graphic throat cancer image attached to it compared with a label with the worded warning, "Smoking can cause cancer." The same effect can be applied in the opposite case in terms of showing a beautiful picture of a healthy person on a vitamin drink compared with the same vitamin drink with a short blurb on its label stating, "This drink will make you healthy." Thus, seeing is believing.

Case

In February 1995, Nick Leeson, a trader for Barings Bank, single-handedly caused the financial collapse of a storied British bank that had been in existence for hundreds of years (known as the "rogue trader" case). Leeson was dealing in risky financial derivatives in the Singapore office (Southeast Asia) of Barings Bank. As the lone trader in Singapore then, Leeson invested heavily on both the Singapore (SIPEX) and Japanese Nikkei exchange indexes. Barings Bank then decided to enter the expanding futures/options business in Asia. Leeson requested to set up and oversee both the accounting and settlement functions for Barings' Singapore branch, as well as for the (same) branch's direct trading floor operations. The London office granted his request, despite the apparent lack of checks and balances, in which Leeson would singularly oversee both the business and operations side of the branch. After receiving Barings' seal of approval, Leeson then headed the Singapore office in 1992.

Initially, Leeson could only execute trades on behalf of clients for "arbitrage trading" purposes (a certain type of trade in which a financial product is bought in one market and then sold in another market for a higher price). After a series of financial successes for Barings, Leeson was then allowed to place orders on behalf of his own account (known as proprietary trading) as well as those on behalf of his clients.

Even after given the right to trade on his own account (the business side of the bank branch), Leeson still supervised accounting and settlements (the operations side of the same bank branch). Because of Leeson's unique position to oversee both sides of the branch, there was no direct oversight or check-and-balance of his trading profit and losses. This allowed Leeson to set up a "dummy" account (several, consecutive "8 digits") in which to funnel what was an emerging series of trading losses. From the perspective of the London office of Barings, Leeson was highly profitable (referred to as being "in the money"). As such, Barings' London office rarely questioned Leeson's series of requests for additional funds, which was used by Leeson to cover his growing losses. In increasingly riskier moves to recover his losses, Leeson took on larger and larger financial positions in the market. Despite Leeson's desperate efforts to dig out of the hole, his losses continued to swell akin to a house of cards.

In January 1995, a huge earthquake hit Japan, sending its financial markets spiraling downward. The Japanese Nikkei crashed, which adversely affected Leeson's position. It was only then that he tried to hedge his positions, but it was too late. By late February, Leeson had lost $1.4 billion. Barings, the bank that financed the Louisiana Purchase between the United States and France, became insolvent and was sold to a competing bank for just one US dollar.

This case of the "rogue trader" demonstrates that even among seemingly sophisticated and smart individuals like Leeson of Baring (who in theory should have acted rationally when handling money in serious situations) could stand to benefit from recognizing his own cognitive illusions and biases – in the form of overconfidence, illusory correlation, prospect theory, endowment effect, denomination fallacy, and failure to recognize the law of large numbers (and reversion to the mean).

Having done so may have helped Barings and Leeson (among other banking scandals to follow) from losing more than a billion dollars that ultimately brought down a historic financial powerhouse.

Bibliography

Albert, S, & Kessler, S 1978, 'Ending Social Encounters', *Journal of Experimental Social Psychology*, vol. 14, no. 16, pp. 541–553. Available from: Elsevier. [5 January 2018].

Carmon, Z, & Ariely, D 2000, 'Focusing in the Forgone: How Value Can Appear so Different to Buyers and Sellers', *Journal of Consumer Research*. Available from: http://citeseerx.ist.psu.edu/viewdoc/download?doi=10.1.1.20.2961&rep=rep1&type=pdf. [25 October 2017].

Defeyter, MA, Russo, R, & McPartlin, PL 2009, 'The Picture Superiority Effect in Recognition Memory: A Development Study Using the Response Signal Procedure', *Cognitive Development*, vol. 24, no. 3, pp. 265–273. Available from: Elsevier. [27 October 2017].

Hamilton, DL, & Gifford, RK 1976, 'Illusory Correlation in Interpersonal Perception: A Cognitive Basis of Stereotypic Judgments', *Journal of Experimental Social Psychology*, vol. 12, no. 4, pp. 392–407. Available from: Elsevier. [25 October 2017].

Hastorf, AH, & Cantril, H 1954, 'They Saw a Game: A Case Study', *Journal of Abnormal Psychology*, vol. 49, no. 1, pp. 129–134. Available from: Psychology Journal Article Collection. [28 October 2017].

Heath, C, & Heath, D 2006, 'The Curse of Knowledge', *Harvard Business Review*. Available from: https://hbr.org/2006/12/the-curse-of-knowledge;at/1. [25 October 2017].

Hoffman, J, & Recober, A 2013, 'Migraine and Triggers: Post Hoc Ergo Propter Hoc?', *Current Pain and Headache Reports*, vol. 17, no. 10, p. 370. Available from: Springer Link. [11 November 2017].

Kahneman, D, Fredrickson, BL, Schreiber, CA, & Redelmeier, DA 1993, 'When More Pain Is Preferred to Less: Adding a Better End', *Psychological Science*, vol. 4, no. 6, pp. 401–405. Available from: Sage Journals. [2 January 2018].

Kahneman, D, Knetsch, JL, & Thaler, RH 1991, 'Anomalies: The Endowment Effect, Loss Aversion, and Status Quo Bias, *The Journal of Economic Perspectives*. Available from: www.princeton.edu/~kahneman/docs/Publications/Anomalies_DK_JLK_RHT_1991.pdf. [15 December 2017].

Lim, RG 1997, 'Overconfidence in Negotiation Revisited', *International Journal of Conflict Management*, vol. 8, no. 1, pp. 52–79. Available from: Emerald Insight. [12 November 2017].

Maoz, I, Ward, A, Katz, M, & Ross, L 2002, 'Reactive Devaluation of an "Israeli" vs. Palestinian" Peace Proposal', *Journal of Conflict Resolution*, vol. 46, no. 4, pp. 515–546. Available from: Sage Journals. [7 November 2017].

McGlone, M, & Tofighbakhsh, J 2000, 'Birds of a Feather Flock Conjointly: Rhyme as Reason in Aphorisms', *Psychological Science*, vol. 11, no. 5, p. 424. Available from: Sage Journals. [11 November 2017].

Ross, L, & Stillinger, C 1991, 'Barriers to Conflict Resolution', *Negotiation Journal*, vol. 7, no. 4, pp. 389–404. Available from: Wiley Online Library. [3 January 2018].

Siades, A, Osherson, D, Bonini, N, & Viale, R 2002, 'On the Reality of the Conjunction Fallacy', *Memory & Cognition*, vol. 30, no. 2, pp. 191–198. Available from: Springer Link. [25 November 2017].

Weber, M, & Camerer, CF 1998, 'The Disposition Effect in Securities Trading: An Experimental Analysis', *Journal of Economic Behavior & Organization*, vol. 33, no. 2, pp. 167–184. Available from: Elsevier. [5 January 2018].

Zajonic, RB 1968, 'Attitudinal Effects of Mere Exposure', *Journal of Personality and Social Psychology Monograph Supplement*, vol. 9, no. 2, pp. 1–24. Available from: http://web.mit.edu/curhan/www/docs/Articles/biases/9_J_Personality_Social_Psychology_1_%28Zajonc%29.pdf. [2 January 2018].

4 Perceptions
How perceptions bend realities

Perceptions

The real world is often not as clear and categorical as a multiple-choice answer. Instead of stark black-and-white, the real world is often a function of different shades of grey.

This is the case with perception. Much like with our world's constantly changing weather, perception is clear on the best days, but can be extremely murky, variable, and temperamental on other days. In other words, when it comes to perception, there is often not a "one-size-fits-all" answer or approach.

As a way to understand perception, think of the formative educational years of a typical student. Most students are, at many points, assessed by multiple-choice exams, in which students are tasked to choose a single best answer among a handful of similarly situated answers. Underlying this examination and assessment approach is a working assumption that generally only one "correct" answer exists.

This is not to say that such variance in perception is a net good or bad tendency. Rather, part of the art and science of persuasion is for individuals – from esteemed experts to scholarly students – to develop a real-time radar awareness of what surrounds individuals in terms of Behavioralist and Rationalist hidden forces. As such, hidden forces shape and constitute the world that individuals perceive and live in on a daily basis.

When it comes to persuasion, perception can play a powerful and pivotal role, particularly relating to important issues concerning ethics, morality, and fairness.

Ethics

To begin the process of examining ethics, imagine the following thought experiment as described in the following situation:

> *You, the reader, are in San Francisco. The greater San Francisco area, known as the Bay Area, is known for many things, including for its*

rolling hills and iconic trolley cars used by both residents and tour-ists alike. While walking downtown, the reader suddenly notices a trol-ley car barreling downwards from the top of a steep hill. Upon closer examination, the reader notices that the trolley car's brakes are failing to function properly. Because of this, the trolley is barreling along its path down the hill with increasing velocity, speed, and force.

There are no people in the trolley car itself. But there are five unsuspect-ing people at the bottom on the hill, exactly where the trolley is heading towards. From the reader's current distance, it is not possible to distinguish among the five people (in terms of age, gender, ethnicity, and so on). You, the reader, quickly surmise that if the trolley car continues speeding down its current path, those five people at the bottom of the hill will be killed by the trolley car. However, next to the reader is a lever. The reader quickly assesses that if the lever is pressed, this will then automatically divert the trolley car to a side street (the lever triggers the trolley path to switch in a way that diverts the trolley car from the road it is on now to the side street).

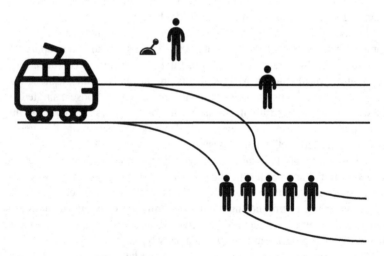

Figure 4.1 Trolley car problem

The reader now faces a literal life-or-death decision – press the lever or not, and based on what reason?

To summarize, here are the choices (choose one, quickly):

A. Press lever; or
B. Do nothing

Write your answer here (A or B): _____

Write your reasoning here:

Now imagine the reader being placed in a similar but slightly different scenario:

> *Everything remains the same as in the original scenario. However, instead of standing next to a lever, the reader is standing on a bridge that overlooks the trolley pathway hurling towards the same five unsuspecting people at the bottom of the hill. Directly in front of you, on the same overpass the reader, is a very large man who is peering down at the pathway. It happens that the large man is facing away from the reader so that the only visible part of him to you is the large man's backside. This means that you, the reader, cannot see the man's face. It then occurs to you that due to the man's sheer size and girth, simply pushing the large man over the bridge would lead to a sufficient blockage of the trolley's pathway to halt the trolley to a full stop, out of harm's way for the five people originally at risk. But doing so would mean that the large man would die as a result.*

The reader now faces a slightly different decision to make – in the next second or two – should the reader push the large man over the bridge or not, and why?

To summarize, here are the choices:

A. Push the large man (over the bridge); or
B. Do nothing

Write your answer here (A or B): _____

Write your reasoning here:

Above and beyond what the reader may have chosen for the two trolley scenarios, the real threshold question is why the reader chose one particular option over another.

The first scenario is known as "The Trolley Problem." It is a classic thought experiment, particularly used by those in the field of philosophy and ethics (Foot 1978; Thomson 1985).

As many readers may have already considered, if answer A were chosen (press lever), then this would result in the loss of one life. However, if B were chosen (do nothing), then this would result in the loss of five lives.

Some readers may then have gone on to make the following calculation: One life versus five lives, which is better (or least worst)? Under this mental metric – which can be thought of as a derivative form of a cognitive cost-benefit analysis – certain readers may have decided that, assuming each life is equal (or roughly equal), it is better to lose one life rather than to lose five lives. Based on this cognitive calculation, by pressing the lever, five lives are saved. Thus, the best (or least worst) choice is to press the lever. Ergo, choice A (press lever).

Often, participants and students placed in this scenario rationalize their choice with statements such as, "It's better to have one person killed than five," "It saves more lives by pressing the lever," and "It's the least worst option since fewer people get killed."

One main underlying tenet (and mental process) relating to such calculation and analysis is the question of what would bring the best result – a version of "utilitarianism" (Mill 1863). Under utilitarianism, the individual should choose the result that brings about the greatest good to the greatest number of people (a derivative form of utility maximization). Utilitarianism can also be viewed as a subset of consequentialism, which posits that the consequences of any action are the determinants of what constitutes right or wrong (Scheffler 1988). In other words, utilitarianism under its traditional definition generally does not outrightly incorporate morality into its calculus.

As brief background, the utilitarianism school of thought was founded by Jeremy Bentham, with its historical roots tracing back to the hedonists, Epicurus and Aristippus, who argued that happiness was the only good to pursue in life. Other utilitarianists included John Stuart Mill, Henry Sidgwick, and Peter Singer, to name a few, who applied the utilitarian school of thought to far-reaching areas, including social justice, global poverty, and the humane treatment of (non-human) animals (Mill 1859; Sidgwick 1981).

What about for those readers who opted *not* to press the lever – what would be your possible reasoning? This leads to the loss of five human lives, when instead, applying utilitarianism, five human lives could have been saved by simply pressing the lever.

Often, participants and students placed in this scenario rationalize their actions by statements such as, "I had no right to decide the fate of those five people," "It was just meant to be for the trolley to go where it was heading," or "The people at the bottom of the trolley's path were just at the wrong place at the wrong time." In an observed setting, most people generally opt to press the lever, with only a minority of participants opting not to do anything (not to press the lever). But why?

Underlying such statements justifying not pressing the lever are moral considerations that can bend perceptions between being a hero and being a murderer. Recall that utilitarianism is generally void of moral considerations and factors. Whatever outcome brings about the greatest happiness, welfare, or utility is the right choice under the utilitarianism purview. However, philosophers such as Immanuel Kant have argued that morality has a place in the decision-making process of individuals – embedded in Kant's "Categorical Imperative" (CI). As such, all immoral actions are irrational since such actions violate CI. In fact, Kant's view is that experience is based on the perception of external objects as well as a priori knowledge. Kant is joined by other philosophers, such as Hobbes and Locke, who also viewed moral requirements as based on standards of rationality. Immanuel Kant further argued that moral requirements were essential to rational agency, and that CI was predicated on humans possessing an innate autonomous will (Kant 1993).

Without such autonomous will and moral component, then the autonomous decision-making process of individuals could arguably be replaced by a relatively straightforward cost-benefit algorithm. Some may not view this in the pejorative, but others may object to the notion that our brain's cognitive function is similar in certain ways to algorithms performing task-oriented goals and roles.

Here, because no one singular "correct" answer arguably exists in this sphere, ethics is inextricably linked to perception in terms of what is perceived as morally "right" or "wrong."

What about for the second iteration of the Trolley Problem involving the large man standing on the bridge?

In this scenario, if individuals – even individuals in highly stressful situations as in the second iteration of the Trolley Problem – were purely rational choice actors in conformity with utilitarianism, arguably most participants should have stayed consistent in terms of trying to maximize utility (in the form of minimizing lives lost) by pushing the large man over the bridge. But interestingly, a tangible shift in the number of participants often occurs in classroom and experiential settings toward the "do nothing" option and away from the take-action option. It's an intriguing shift. But why would such people shift?

Here, the path to the answer bends again to perception. Participants and students placed in this second iteration of the Trolley Problem attempted to rationalize their new decision ("do nothing" choice) with statements such as, "It just felt wrong to push the man over the bridge," "I didn't want to be the one responsible for the killing of a person," and "It's just different to push a man over a bridge than to just push a lever – it's almost murder."

The outcome (consequence of such action) is, of course, the same. So strictly speaking, because utilitarianism is linked to consequentialism, then only the bottom line should matter, at least in theory. This view may hold true if humans were simple cost-benefit–calculating creatures. But nonetheless, based on such evidence and responses, it could be that something in the human condition invokes a certain moral code, albeit learned and/ or inherent in our genetic makeup, for some when it comes to a direct and physical pushing of a person compared with the simple pressing of a lever or button – again, noting that the consequences are irrefutably identical.

Such phenomena give rise to some very interesting, and arguably, concerning considerations in our modern era, increasingly driven by decision-making algorithms and autonomous technology, from self-driving cars to autonomous drones.

Other ethical concerns can arise in negotiations and deal-making. When trying to determine whether an action or behavior is ethical or not, two fundamental questions can help determine what is the right thing to do: (1) Do all the parties know and agree to the standard of conduct being used? and (2) Do all the parties have freedom to enter into and leave the negotiation? If both answers are "yes," then this may be evidence of sound ethical behavior and conduct. If a "no" answer exists somewhere, then conversely, this may be evidence of unethical behavior and conduct (Lax & Sebenius 2007).

Other driving questions exist related to ethics. First, if the parties were able to see themselves, would they find such conduct acceptable or not, and why? Second, if the type of behavior being used was leveraged against the party using it, would this be viewed as acceptable or not? Third, if a party advised others on what type of behavior to use, what type of behavior would be recommended as acceptable, and why? Fourth, if a party was tasked to design a system (model rules) of ethical conduct, would the contemplated conduct be the model one? Fifth, would society as a whole gain and be better off from the conduct being used? Sixth, do other alternative tactics exist that could accomplish the same goal? Seventh, and finally, when taking a broader (meta) view of the behavior or tactic being used, would such conduct still be viewed favorably? (Lax & Sebenius 2007).

From a big-picture perspective, the concept of ethics can be juxtapositioned with the concepts of emotion and economics. These three concepts – ethics, emotion, and economics – is referred to by me as the 3E Principle in negotiations. Each of the three Es can be given a particular percentage weighting whereby the three Es added together equal 100 percent. For example, one person may view profit as paramount, thus leading to a 3E Principle weighting of, say, economics (50 percent), ethics (20 percent), and emotion (30 percent). Another person working for a non-profit organization may alternatively view ethics as paramount, thus leading to a 3E Principle weighting of, say, ethics (60 percent), emotion (25 percent), and economics (15 percent).

3E principle

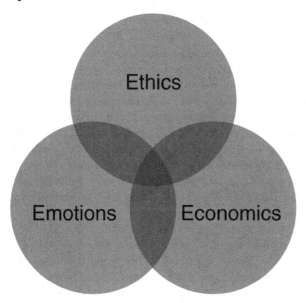

Figure 4.2 (3E Principle)

Separate but related from ethical concerns is the perception of fairness, discussed next.

Fairness

What is or should be "fair"? The issue of what exactly constitutes "fair" versus "unfair" underlies many spheres of influence – from academic circles to political public policy debates. Generally, most people would probably agree that being fair is the "right thing to do." But this then again strikes at the very core of exactly what constitutes "fair" versus "unfair."

The 2008 subprime crisis, for example, led many to question what was fair in terms of how homeowners were treated by certain unscrupulous mortgage lenders, at the micro level, and how wealth should be distributed (or redistributed), at the macro level in terms of income equality.

So what is the "right" answer? As with ethics, fairness is bound by perception. In other words, fairness, much like ethics, is a perception game. If "beauty is in the eye of the beholder," then arguably, the determinants underlying fairness is also "in the eye of the beholder." Thus, understanding fairness is subjective as well as objective, dependent on the particular individual or society in question.

To illustrate this point, imagine another thought experiment in which the reader is suddenly and unexpectedly placed in the following scenario:

You, the reader, are sitting in a nice university cafe. You are drinking a hot, frothy cappuccino, enjoying some "quality reading time." It is a very pleasant day. Because of the nice day, the cafe is bustling with people, which includes some people sitting near and around you. While sitting and reading, you happen to notice a pleasant-looking couple smiling and walking in a beeline directly toward you. At first, you do not pay any particular attention to them. But after a while, it becomes clear that the couple is intent on walking straight toward you to talk. You glance up to get a better look at the approaching couple. To your surprise, the couple is none other than Bill and Melinda Gates (of the Bill and Melinda Gates Foundation).

Melinda Gates speaks first. She says, "Hi there! I'm Melinda and this is my husband, Bill. To give you a little background, Bill and I run a philanthropic organization. And we're super passionate about effective, evidence-based philanthropy. So we're trying to find the most effective and efficient ways possible to maximize good for society. And we'd like your help! As part of our effective philanthropy mission, we run various social experiments. If you're up for it, as part of one such social experiment, we'd like to give you $100. You don't have to pay any of it back. The only thing we ask in exchange for the $100 is for you to make a decision: How much, if any, of the $100 would you choose to give to that person over there?" (Assume you keep any amount not given and that the person who is the potential receiver knows you were given $100 to give or not to give.)

She then points to a person sitting a few tables away from you (assume this person, the potential receiver, has heard everything that Melinda has said to you). You do not know the person Melinda is pointing to, but you surmise that the other person is probably affiliated in some way with the local university.

You, the reader, now have to make a decision – in the next couple of seconds: How much of the $100, if any, to give?

Write your answer here (any figure from $0 to $100):

Amount given: $_____

Why did you give this amount? (Write your short answer below):

Now suppose the reader is placed in a slightly different scenario. The facts remain the same as in the first scenario, but with one stark difference: the receiver can say "yes" or "no" to your proposed (offered) amount. If the receiver says "yes" to your offered amount, then both you and the receiver will get the agreed-upon amounts. But, if the receiver says "no" to your offered amount, then neither you nor the receiver receives anything (you both get $0). (Assume again that the reader keep any amount not given if accepted, and that the receiver is aware that you were given $100 to give or not give to the receiver.)

The reader now must make a decision – again, in the next couple of seconds: How much of the $100, if any, to give?

Write your answer here (any figure from $0 to $100):

Amount to give: $_____

Why did you give this amount? (Write your short answer below):

The original scenario is an experiential exercise, referred to as the "Dictator Game." The Dictator Game is named as such since the amount given is decided entirely by the giver (you the reader) at your sole and absolute discretion. The receiver has no choice but to take what was given, no matter how large or small, similar to the plight of the people in a dictatorship (Kahneman, Knetsch & Thaler 1986).

The Dictator Game tries to answer the question, "What is fair?" Most reasonable people will generally agree that a "fair" amount should be given (in a negotiation, social policy, or other related setting). But the more critical and exacting question is how the term and concept of exactly what is "fair" (and unfair) translates into action from different people's perspectives based on potential (known and unknown) perceptions.

Is what is "fair" always mutually clear and agreed upon – or is fairness, figuratively and literally, lost in translation?

The second scenario is a derivative of the Dictator Game, referred to as the "Ultimatum Game." Here, the receiver is not playing a passive role (as in the Dictator Game), but an active role since the receiver has the freedom to choose whether to accept or reject your (the giver's) offered amount (Andersen, Ertaç, Gneezy, Hoffman & List 2011).

Before turning to the actual research results, it is important to examine the underlying theory related to the Dictator and Ultimatum Games. Doing so will provide a method to compare what people "ought" to do (in theory) in relation to what people "actually did do" (in practice).

In theory, specifically under rational choice theory (RCT), what should be the minimum amount that should be accepted (by the receiver) in the Ultimatum Game?

If the reader guessed "anything above $0," then this would be what most Rationalists would deem as the correct answer. After all, under rational choice theory, any amount that the receiver receives above zero is an amount that the receiver did not have originally. So, for this reason, the receiver ought to accept any amount based on such purported sense and sensibility, at least in theory – devoid of pride and prejudice. This would include accepting amounts as low as $0.01 (out of $100).

But does this comport with research results among actual people, in practice?

The short answer is no. It turns out that – in contrast to rational choice theory – the rejection rates of participants placed in the Ultimatum Game became particularly pronounced at about $30 and lower (out of $100) being offered. What could explain such behavior? Often the feedback comes in the form of, "Well, the amount didn't seem fair compared to what the giver had," "I expected half and didn't get half," and "The giver didn't do anything for the $100, so I should have gotten more."

So what is to be concluded based on the Trolley Problem and the Dictator/ Ultimatum Games? One takeaway could be that certain people do not always prescribe and conform to how individuals "ought" to act under rational choice theory. Some people are instead influenced by behavioral hidden forces. After all, Behavioralists and Rationalists both live in the real world.

This leaves the door open to persuasion as a function of perception within issues of ethics and fairness – critical issues that often cannot simply and monolithically be compartmentalized into "one-size-fits-all" answers for all people in all situations. In sum, perceptions persuade people.

Case

The dawn of a new era where autonomous-driving vehicles will dominate the streets is fast approaching. Tesla Motors, founded by Elon Musk, helped to usher in an era where the decisions made by humans have increasingly, and perhaps inevitably, been replaced by algorithms and artificial intelligence (AI).

Some hold the view that algorithms and AI cannot replace humans, no matter how sophisticated the technology. Based on this view, humans have an uncanny and unique ability to gauge driving situations that will be of most benefit for both the driver and society-at-large in terms of safety and collision rates. Moreover, under this view, past car accidents (albeit relatively few in number) of near-autonomous driving vehicles represent clear, demonstrable proof of the fallibility of the future of self-driving cars.

Those on the other side will counter-argue that accidents involving self-driving cars are rare, isolated events. Moreover, while AI is not exactly flawless, nor are humans as drivers flawless – as evidenced by human errors involved in car accidents, particularly when drivers are intoxicated, drowsy, or preoccupied. Moreover, under this argument, one tangible benefit of autonomous vehicles driven (literally) by algorithms and AI is that their processing systems can learn and gather data extremely efficiently, at a level rivaling or exceeding those of humans.

A middle-path view is that humans and their technological counterparts are not mutually exclusive and can peacefully co-exist. After all, it is humans (so far) who are programming the machines. Thus, precautions and stop-gap measures can be placed by human programmers into the processing systems of autonomous-driving vehicles.

This then leads to an interesting dilemma involving ethics, morality, and fairness (as evidenced earlier with the Trolley Problem and Dictator/Ultimatum Games). Imagine a scenario involving a self-driving car operating at night that suddenly spots three people directly in front of it who had for whatever reason wandered into the middle of the road. If the self-driving car continues forward along its present path, it will kill all three people. However, if the driver presses a lever on the car's instrument panel, the car's algorithm will divert the vehicle to the nearest alternate path. But in this scenario, the nearest alternate path involves a young child on the street who will certainly be killed (instead of the three people who wandered onto the road originally).

What would you do if you were the driver? Let the self-driving car continue (killing three people), or press the button (and kill a young child)? Is this the right thing to do for all drivers in the same or similar situation?

Next, assume instead that you are the algorithm (human) programmer for the self-driving car. Would you program the algorithm to continue forward or have the algorithm press the button automatically in such a situation, and why?

The only clear aspect concerning such profound questions – interlinking perception, ethics, morality, and fairness – is that their answers are anything but clear.

Bibliography

Andersen, S, Ertaç, S, Gneezy, U, Hoffman, M, & List, JA 2011, 'Stakes Matter in Ultimatum Games', *The American Economic Review*, vol. 101, no. 7, pp. 3427–3439. Available from: Jstor. [5 January 2018].

Foot, P 1978, 'The Problem of Abortion and the Doctrine of the Double Effect in Virtues and Vices', *Oxford Review*, vol. 5, pp. 5–15. Available from: PhilPapers. [12 December 2017].

Kahneman, D, Knetsch, JL, & Thaler, RH 1986, 'Fairness and the Assumptions of Economics', *The Journal of Business*, vol. 59, no. 4, pp. 285–300. Available from: Jstor. [2 January 2018].

Kant, I 1993, *Grounding for the Metaphysics of Moral*, 3rd edn, Hackett Publishing Company, Cambridge, UK.

Lax, D, & Sebenius, J 2007, 'Three Ethical Issues in Negotiation', *Negotiation Journal*, vol. 2, no. 4. Available from: Wiley Online Library. [5 January 2018].

Mill, JS 1859, *On Liberty*, Dover Publications, Mineola, NY.

Mill, JS 1863, *Utilitarianism*, Batoche Books Limited, Ontario.

Scheffler, S 1988, *Consequentialism and Its Critics*, Oxford University Press, Oxford.

Sidgwick, H 1981, *Methods of Ethics*, 7th edn, Hackett Publishing Company, Cambridge, UK.

Thomson, JJ 1985, 'The Trolley Problem', *The Yale Law Journal*, vol. 94, no. 6, pp. 1395–1415. Available from: Jstor. [25 October 2017].

Part II

Rationalists

Sense and sensibility

5 Strategies
Knowing when to keep calm
and carry on

Prisoner's dilemma

Imagine being placed in the following situation whereby a strategy must be chosen.

> *Two people – A and B – are co-workers. They want to make a quick buck. So they conspire to steal money from their company through cyberhacking of the company's financial database. After some planning, A and B then move forward on their plan to steal money from the company online. Ultimately, however, A and B are unsuccessful and thereafter caught by the police. The two individuals – A and B – are then taken to the local police department for interrogation in separate cells (prison rooms) related to their alleged cybercrime. The police first question Prisoner A. The police inform Prisoner A that if A confesses, A can go home free from jail right away. But if A chooses not to confess, then A will spend several years in jail (based on electronic evidence collected from the cybercrime).*

Should Prisoner A cooperate or not with the police, and why exactly? Does a strategy exist to make this important decision? And if so, is there a strategy that beats all other strategies?

Such threshold questions do not make for an easy and elementary analysis for the uninitiated. As some readers may know, the preceding scenario is a much-beloved fact pattern underlying a thought experiment referred to as the Prisoner's Dilemma (PD). Prisoner's Dilemma is a game theory scenario in which game players, often two or more in number, must choose between betrayal or cooperation with one another. PD is predicated on, among other things, the players acting fully rationally (Neumann & Morgenstern 1953). PD is often utilized as a conceptual exercise to demonstrate the notion of how to rationally and strategically decide among and between two options – in this case, betrayal or cooperation – applying a semblance of a structured and systematic strategic method.

To get to the answer, the following sections will apply a GPS framework:

- G: What are the Game rules?
- P: What are the Payouts?
- S: What is the best Strategy?

Dominant strategy

As a prelude to the actual analysis of what would be A's best *Strategy (S)*, many reasons can be given to cooperate or betray. These reasons can range from loyalty to pure selfish interests, and variances in between. But the central question, from a strategy standpoint, is: Does a strategy exist that is better than any other strategy, no matter what B does, assuming that A acts fully rationally and is only concerned about minimizing A's jail time?

This issue strikes at the core of a concept known as *dominant strategy (DS)* – a strategy that is better than any other strategy, or alternatively, the strategy with the best payouts (Turocy & Stengel 2001). Applying the concept of dominant strategy helps to cut and clarify exactly what is (and is not) the best (dominant) strategy in this or other similarly situated PD scenarios.

Here, the dominant strategy is to betray. But why is betraying, rather than cooperating, A's dominant strategy?

To help with the analysis, below is a matrix outlining the aforementioned PD scenario (Figure 5.1). It is a four-quadrant matrix whereby each prisoner has the identical (symmetrical) binary options of either betraying or cooperating. Within each of the four quadrants are the number of prison years that will be the outcome based on the decisions of the two prisoners (the upper-right corner figure reflects time spent in jail for Prisoner A; the lower-left corner figure reflects time spent in jail for Prisoner B).

The Prisoner's Dilemma also relies on the following sweeping academic assumptions (be ready to take a big breath before reading):

- Both prisoners are acting rationally
- Both prisoners are unable to communicate with each other
- Both prisoners do not fear retribution by the other prisoner
- Both prisoners cannot control the actions of the other prisoner
- Both prisoners only have one chance to make a decision (called a "non-iterated" event)

Prisoner's dilemma

	Confess A	Stay quiet A
Confess **B**	6 6	10 0
Stay quiet **B**	0 10	2 2

Figure 5.1 Prisoner's dilemma

From A's perspective, looking at the Payouts matrix, let's simply compare A's Payouts (P) when A betrays (confesses) relative to when A cooperates (stays quiet), referring to Figure 5.1, the PD-related Payouts (Points) diagram. When A confesses and B confesses (upper-left box), A spends six years in jail (upper right corner of the same box). However, if A had instead stayed quiet while B confessed (upper-right box), A would have spent ten years in jail (instead of six) (upper-right corner of the same box). Thus, A is better off betraying (in terms of Payouts) in this case (since A would receive six years in jail by betraying rather than ten years in jail by staying quiet).

Next, if A confesses and B stays quiet (lower-left box), then A spends zero years in jail and B spends ten years in jail. However, if A had instead cooperated while B also cooperated (lower-right box), then A would have spent two years (as would have B) (upper-right corner of the same box). Thus, A is again better off betraying in this case (since A would have received zero years in jail by betraying rather than two years in jail by staying quiet). The culmination of A's outcomes yield the same conclusion: A is better off again betraying (in terms of Payouts) in this case.

Putting both (all) possible scenarios together: A is *always* better off by confessing, no matter what B does. Thus, A's dominant strategy (DS) is to confess – based on these particular PD payouts.

What is B's dominant strategy then? The short answer is: Betray.

The important point here – since Payouts can and often do change in theory and practice – is not merely to memorize that betrayal "is" the right answer in this specific case. Rather, the point is to understand "why" betraying (in this particular case, based on these particular Payouts) represents the dominant strategy.

Specifically, from Prisoner B's perspective, looking at the Payouts matrix again, when B confesses and A confesses (upper-left box), B spends six years in jail (lower-left of the same box). However, if B had instead stayed quiet while A confessed (lower-left box), B would have instead spent ten years in jail (lower-left of the same box). Thus, B is again better off confessing in this case (since B would receive six years by betraying instead of ten years in jail by staying quiet).

Next, if B confesses and A stays quiet (upper-right box), B spends zero years in jail (lower-left of the same box). However, if both B and A had cooperated (lower-right box), B would have spent two years in jail (lower-left corner of the same box). Thus, B is again better off betraying in this case (since B would receive zero years by betraying rather than two years in jail by staying quiet).

Thus, B's dominant strategy is to confess. Putting it all together, both Prisoners A and B have the same DS of betraying – thus, they should each (both) confess to the police. Betraying, in other words, would be a strategy that beats any other strategy, for both A and B, individually.

This brings to light an added interesting PD feature. The Payouts matrix box in which both A and B betray is the box that is best for each individual (A and B; $2 + 2 = 4$). However, it has the *worst* (maximum) payouts ($6 + 6 = 12$) for both players together as a group. Thus, what is best for the individual's pursuit of individual self-gain – also known as rational behavior – represents the worst for the group (which can alternatively be referred to as "society," "community," or "country"). This is what is referred to as the "*tragedy of the commons*" in which the maximization of individual gain can lead to the seemingly sudden rise and fall of great societies and even empires (Hardin 1968).

Would this then imply that betrayal is always the best (dominant) strategy?

Betrayal may be the best strategy *in this case*, assuming all of its academic assumptions exist. For instance, all players must act rationally (in a pure cost-benefit analysis unimpeded by emotion or context at all times). Second, the scenario is a one-time (non-iterated) event. This means that factors such as feelings for a person or the opportunity to seek retorsion for previous actions are not typically incorporated into the Game Rules within the GPS framework. This may seem acceptable academically. But for many practitioners, such academic leaps of faith may seem downright dubious.

As alluded to previously, PD is part of an academic discipline known as game theory. As the term denotes, the exercise of finding a dominant strategy is often a useful first step in persuasion and negotiation strategy. However, because of the constraints of PD's working assumptions, its strategic framework should not be the first and last steps in a strategic context. Despite this, versions of PD – using supercomputers and inclusion of a myriad of data points – have been used in very serious real-world contexts, such as during the Cold War (to the present day) to decide whether betrayal (in the form of a military and/or nuclear weapons first strike) or cooperation (no military and/or nuclear first strike) would represent a dominant strategy (Poundstone 1993). If it serves as any assurance, the fact that the world is not yet entered into full-scale nuclear war may be the most clear evidence that, at least so far, the relevant countries have opted for cooperation as their dominant strategy (if, for no other reason, than fear of full retaliatory retribution in an iterated PD scenario).

Mutually assured destruction and tit-for-tat

The previous PD scenario had Payouts such that betrayal was the dominant strategy. But what are its possible ramifications – not just in the short run, but the long run as well? Shifting semantics slightly, a betrayal-betrayal option and outcome by both players could be reframed as a lose-lose outcome, referred to as a Mutually Assured Destruction (MAD) (Sokolski 2004). Assuming a purely and perfectly rational world, cooler heads and rational decision-making would prevail, and thus, always prevent MAD outcomes (such as in nuclear war by two superpowers). However, while this may be true in many or even most cases, as other chapters of this book describe in greater detail, consistent and reliable rational behavior may not always exist in perfect form at all times.

Rather than MAD, the literature suggests that the best strategy in this scenario (or Game rules) is Tit-for-Tat (TFT). In the TFT framework – a form of PD strategy – underlying an iterated Prisoner's Dilemma game, players should start the initial round in a PD game scenario by signaling cooperation. Thereafter, a tit-for-tat mirroring strategy should be employed. For example, in Week 2 of an iterated PD game scenario, Player A would cooperate if Player B cooperated (after cooperating in the initial round or iteration). However, and conversely, Player A would betray if Player B betrayed. Thereafter, in Week 3, the same strategy would ensue of mirroring the other player until the final round. This TFT strategy in an iterated PD framework allows for punishment (sticks) for bad behavior (betrayal), while also providing incentives (carrots) for good behavior (cooperation) (Axelrod 1985).

TFT may be the dominant strategy in a game theory framework. But as academically elegant as the PD game theory framework may appear to some, its weaknesses arise in at least two areas.

First, although the TFT strategy may be the *relatively* better strategy, this does not mean that TFT is the optimal strategy on an absolute basis. In other words, to use economics jargon, TFT may lead to non-optimal equilibrium (outcomes). Second, the PD game framework assumes that game players are always fully "rational" (by maximizing one's own benefit only and conforming to transitivity). However, as the first section of this book describes, the assumption that actors are always fully rational at all times in every contextual situation is counter to the academic findings of many behavioral scientists and economists (Shiller 2015).

Strategic points

Mutually Assured Destruction (MAD) represents a worst-case, lose-lose scenario. But how do players devise a strategy for better relative and absolute results (payouts)?

In an ideal world, persuasion-based negotiation strategies should lead to more positive potential results. Often such results are a function of strategy in a negotiation context whereby both sides are effectively communicating, verbally and/or nonverbally, with one another. The objective of both sides should be to get to a point, or range of points, where the parties are better off saying yes to a deal with one another (cooperating) – rather than saying no and not dealing with one another (betraying).

Such concept is referred to as the Zone of Possible Agreement (ZOPA). It is a strategy that helps answer the question of whether to say "yes" or "no" to an offer – notably based on rational behavior.

Finding ZOPA involves the following strategic steps.

Reservation points

The first step is to know two walkaway points: (1) Party A's walkaway point and (2) Party B's walkaway point. Suppose that Party A is a buyer and that Party B is a seller. The technical term for such a walkaway point is a Reservation Point (RP) (Korobkin 2000). Reservation Points are then subdivided into the Buyer's RP and the Seller's RP. The Buyer's RP is the maximum point that the Buyer is willing to pay (as distinguishable from what the Buyer can pay) for a particular good or service. The Buyer's RP assumes that the Buyer is willing to accept anything below the Buyer's RP (since a buyer should accept paying anything less than the maximum point for a good or service, at least from a Rationalist's standpoint). The Seller's RP is, in contrast to the Buyer's RP, the minimum point that the Seller is willing to sell (as distinguishable from what the Seller can sell) for a particular good or service. The Seller's RP assumes that the Seller is willing to accept anything above the Seller's Reservation Point (since the seller should accept receiving anything more than the minimum point for a good or service, at least from a Rationalist's standpoint).

To apply this principle, consider the following example: Imagine Party A (Buyer) is considering purchasing a home. As the Buyer, Party A's strategic issue would be the maximum price that Party A is willing to pay (WTP) for a home. This point represents the Buyer's RP. Assume now that, everything considered and after careful consideration, the Buyer determines that its (Buyer's) RP is $700,000. This completes step one.

The next step is to calculate Party B's (Seller's) walkaway point (as the home seller). In other words, what would be the minimum price that the Seller would be willing to sell this particular home on the market. This point represents the Seller's RP.

At this point, assume it is often generally unknown exactly what the Seller's RP may be from the Buyer's standpoint (particularly in the real world). As a stop-gap measure, the Buyer should seek and incorporate all available information. Based on such available information, the Buyer should then make best efforts to calculate the Seller's RP, which may entail making working assumptions. Thus, for purposes of applying the RP concept in this example, assume that everything considered based on all available information, the Seller's RP is determined to be $400,000.

So far, based on the given facts, the following has been calculated (based on perfect or imperfect information, as the case may be):

- RP Buyer (maximum point) = $700,000
- RP Seller (minimum point) = $400,000

The next strategic issue in this simulated scenario is: Does a point, or range of points, exist whereby both parties are better off saying "yes" than "no," in this particular case?

The short answer is yes – specifically, it is the range of price points between $400,000 and $700,000 (inclusive). The "yesable" points represent the Zone of Possible Agreement (ZOPA). Within ZOPA, every point represents a point in which both parties are better off saying "yes" than "no" – based primarily on the edicts of rational behavior.

Insult zones

Extending the ZOPA strategic framework further, at the extreme ends of price points for the parties are defining the parties' possible Insult Zones. These Insult Zones are points that are perceived as so extreme or egregious by the counterparty that it triggers a walkout from the negotiation table (and refusal to enter into further negotiations).

So what could constitute entering into the Insult Zone with the previous home purchase and sale example? An offered price of $1 by the Buyer for the Seller's home may potentially enter the Seller's Insult Zone since it would be an extreme low-offer bid. Note that calculating Insult Zones represents more of an art than a science based on the degree of rationality employed by the parties. The Seller, for instance, may take the view that the

$1 extreme low offer is merely the beginning of an expected "buyer bids high, seller bids low" haggle in which extreme bargaining is part of the negotiation process. However, the risk is that the Seller may instead view the Buyer's extreme "low-ball" offer as a personal attack or affront on either the home and/or the Seller. Such mindset may not be fully rational, but it may arguably be part of the human condition as social animals. In such cases, non-economic, emotional attachment and value is often placed on a particular good or service, knowingly or unknowingly.

Related to the ZOPA strategic framework, a "negotiation dance" can occur. A negotiation dance is a negotiation process that involves bargained-for points that can include ZOPA (which again, represents the range of "yes-able" points) – but generally does not enter (exists outside) the Insult Zones of Buyer and Seller. These points are referred to as Bargaining Zones (BZ). A Bargaining Zone is a point, or range of points, that the Buyer and Seller believe has a reasonable likelihood of getting to yes, if the parties continue to negotiate (which can be inclusive of ZOPA).

Putting it all together – Buyer's RP, Seller's RP, ZOPA, Bargaining Zones, and Insult Zones – is the following simple schematic (Figure 5.2):

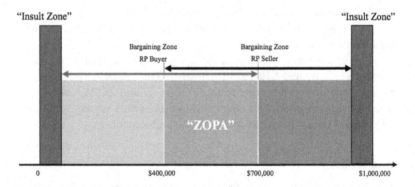

Figure 5.2 Zones

With the ZOPA framework, the information used for each of the various points may or may not represent perfect information (as would be assumed in a purely theoretical analysis). Thus, the foregoing analyses, particularly regarding RPs and ZOPA, should be viewed as a strategic starting point, but not necessarily an ending point of a given strategic analysis. This means that as additional information is obtained, the various strategic points described previously can and should be constantly calibrated and adjusted.

Strategic information

At a more macro level, when entering strategic decision-making, how does a party know what information to seek or not to seek? After all, in the current Google era where information is instantly available, parties may find themselves in a crisis of too much information (rather than too little information, as was the case in the pre-internet era).

Information is critically important in a persuasion and negotiation context. Often the party that has relatively more informational power will also have greater negotiation power, and thus, be in more of a position to dictate the bargaining process and outcome. Because fear can be driven by the unknown, more information helps to lower fear in a negotiation context. Lower fear levels, in turn, often translate to lower risk perception, and thus, help to increase (but not guarantee) higher levels of cooperation among the parties.

As such, an added strategic approach to sift through either an abyss or overabundance of information is through the following Information Matrix (Figure 5.3). The Information Matrix is similar to a search engine keyword filter that aims to provide better and more relevant information for analysis.

Specifically, two types of information exist at the macro level (see Figure 5.3): Known Information and Unknown Information. If we assume that these two types of information exist for two parties, then we can view the types of information schematically into four sub-sets: (1) Known-Known Information (upper-left box); (2) Unknown-Known Information (lower-left box); (3) Known-Unknown Information (upper-right box); and (4) Unknown-Unknown Information (lower-right box).

Information matrix

	Known Information	Unknown Information
Known Information	Known-Known Information	Known-Unknown Information
Unknown Information	Unknown-Known Information	Unknown-Unknown Information

Figure 5.3 (Information Matrix)

Descriptions for each of the four Information Matrix boxes follow:

First, Known-Known Information is information which parties know that they know. For example, the current stock price of a particular company or the number of missiles of a particular state could represent Known-Known variables. Second, Known-Unknown Information is information which parties know that they do not know. For example, the stock price of a particular company or number of missiles of a particular state ten years from now could represent Known-Unknown variables. Third, Unknown-Known Information is information which parties do not know that they know. For example, the inability of a company to create value out of its currently existing resources, or the inability of a regime to invent new military technology based on currently existing technology or resources, could represent Unknown-Known variables. Fourth, and finally, Unknown-Unknown Information is information which parties do not know that they do not know (implying variables that have not been given previous strategic thought). For example, the internet, AI, or driverless cars a century ago could be examples of Unknown-Unknown information.

In conclusion, persuasion and negotiation theory and practice represent a function of strategy. Such strategies are based on information and frameworks, such as PD, GPS, DS, MAD, TFT, ZOPA, RP, Insult Zones, Bargaining Zones, and the Information Matrix.

Case

Assume two hypothetical provinces exist – Alphaville and Betaville – within the same country, Shangri-La. Alphaville's historical specialization is in the production of bread. Betaville's historical specialization is in the production of smartphones. All is well, until unexpectedly and suddenly, a virus outbreak ensues and starts to spread across the country of Shangri-La, invariably entering into the provinces of both Alphaville and Betaville. Because of the sudden and seemingly dangerous virus outbreak, both provinces decide to switch production to Vaccine X. Under a national emergency decree, Shangri-La declares that only Alphaville and Betaville are allowed to produce Vaccine X in the country, and that the two provinces should sell Vaccine X through an electronic (online) seller's system. A total of eight online sell sessions will occur once every week for the next eight weeks. Each online weekly sell session will consist of online bids that represent separately submitted Vaccine X sell prices set by both Alphaville and Betaville to potential buyers domestically and globally. The sell sessions will occur simultaneously (both provinces will submit their online bids at the same time). In the selling session system, for simplicity, only three bidding price options exist: $10, $20, or $30, for both provinces.

If both provinces charge the same amount (Alphaville: $10 and Betaville: $10; Alphaville: $20 and Betaville: $20; or Alphaville: $30 and Betaville: $30), then each province receives the same amount of profit for that particular sell session. Profit is needed for each province's financial stimulus program since the virus outbreak has caused financial market panic.

Assume that the maximum profit for both provinces is attained when each/both set $30 as the session's sell price, followed by $20, and then $10 bid amounts by each side. However, if one province undercuts the other province, the undercutting province receives more profit (at the expense of the non-undercutting province receiving less profit for that particular bid session). For example, in Week 1's bid, if Betaville sets a selling price of $20, but Alphaville sets a selling price of $10, then Alphaville will earn more profit for that bid week (since more buyers will opt for the relatively lower-priced $10 Vaccine X product).

Here, the two options would be: Cooperate or Betray (Non-Cooperation). What would be the dominant strategy (DS) in this scenario – for Alphaville, Betaville, and both provinces collectively?

Suppose the reader is selected to be part of Alphaville's strategy team for the upcoming eight-week selling sessions. What should be the advise given to Alphaville (sell at $10, $20, or $30, and based on what specific strategy)? Does enough information exist to determine a dominant strategy? Even if a dominant strategy could be determined, would you recommend pursuing it, and why? Would the recommendation be to sell the vaccine at the same price for all eight selling sessions, or not? And what would be the strategic criteria, if any, for changing vaccine prices applying PD, GPS, DS, TFT, MAD, and ZOPA, among other strategies?

Here, much like in the most sophisticated public policy scenarios, a clear one-size-fits-all answer may or may not seem readily apparent. But having strategic frameworks maximizes the opportunity for success.

Bibliography

Axelrod, R 1985, *The Evolution of Cooperation*, Basic Books, New York.

Hardin, G 1968, 'The Tragedy of Commons', *Science*, vol. 162, no. 3859, pp. 1243–1248. Available from: http://science.sciencemag.org/content/162/3859/1243.full. [3 January 2018].

Korobkin, RB 2000, 'A Positive Theory of Legal Negotiation', *Georgetown Law Journal*. Available from: https://papers.ssrn.com/sol3/papers.cfm?abstract_id=221588. [30 November 2017].

Neumann, JV, & Morgenstern, O 1953, *Theory of Games and Economic Behavior*, Princeton University Press, Princeton.

Poundstone, W 1993, *Prisoner's Dilemma: John von Neumann, Game Theory, and the Puzzle of the Bomb*, Anchor Books, New York.

Shiller, RJ 2015, *Irrational Exuberance*, Princeton University Press, Princeton.

Sokolski, HD 2004, *Getting MAD: A Nuclear Mutual Assured Destruction, Its Origins and Practice*, University of California Libraries, Oakland.

Turocy, TL, & Stengel, BV 2001, 'Game Theory', *Encyclopedia of Information Systems*. Available from: www.cdam.lse.ac.uk/Reports/Files/cdam-2001-09.pdf. [22 December 2017].

6 Expectations
How to value great expectations

Rational choice theory

Much of the literature pertaining to persuasion is predicated on critical assumptions that allow the models to function as advertised. One bedrock underlying assumption is that actors within a persuasion context model make "rational" choices.

This then begs the question: What exactly is a so-called rational choice? The Oxford English Dictionary defines "rational" to mean an act or choice that is "based on or in accordance with reason or logic." Without going into granular detail on the many schools of thought, from economics to philosophy, regarding what is and what is not rational per se pursuant to a particular academic perspective, one common unifying theme spanning across various disciplines is that rational behavior is consistent with being transitive in nature.

Transitivity means that if A is preferred to B, and if B is preferred to C, then A should be preferred to C (Regenwetter, Dana & Davis-Stober 2011). That means that preference can be rank-ordered. Moreover, many hold that, pursuant to a transitivity context, such rank-ordering must be both constant and consistent. This means that such preference selection and rank-ordering should not waver, and should not be subject to the whims of non-rational factors (such as biases, cognitive shortcuts, context, or emotions). As such, albeit having a good day or bad day, when an actor renders a particular choice among perfect or imperfect information inputs, the rational actor must always use reason and logic to maximize utility, while staying tenaciously true to transitivity.

The genesis of Rational Choice Theory (RCT) can be traced back to, among other places, the RAND Corporation during the beginning of the Cold War. RCT's original mandate at the RAND Corporation was a response from policy makers to (mathematically) model the decisions of the Soviet Union during the Cold War. This school of thought, which contrasts to the behavioral school of thought, assumes that individual and group (societal) behavior can be explained by the outcome of rational choices made by individual actors. RCT took an early foothold in the field of economics, as seen in Kenneth Arrow's (1951) text, *Social Choice and individual Values*, and went on to dominate the academic landscape at various institutions, such as at the University of Chicago, MIT, and other institutions.

This is the theory on paper. But is this the case in practice? Rather than provide a one-line, one-size-fits-all answer, this chapter provides the tools and evidence necessary for you the reader to begin to make a conclusion independently.

Behavioralism

An alternative school of thought to RCT – Behavioralism (such as behavioral finance and economics) – questions and rebuts the RCT school of thought that all actors are always rational irrespective of contextual dynamics. The Behavioralist school of thought has increasingly gained a foothold among both academics and practitioners, particularly following the 2008 financial crisis, which many believed to be clear prima facie evidence that not all actors behave rationally at all times, particularly during crises (such as when someone yells "Fire!" in a crowded movie theater).

Daniel Kahneman emerged as one of the main proponents of the behavioral model of the world. Kahneman, often working with his colleague, Amos Tversky, began researching and publishing a series of groundbreaking articles that provided evidence – based on actual human conduct – rather than postulative theory alone, that the human mind did not always act in perfect harmony with rational behavior. In this spirit, Kahneman as a social psychologist famously noted that "Economists observe what people should do. Psychologists observe what people actually do" (Kahneman, Slovic & Tversky 1982; Kahneman, Diener & Schwarz 1999; Kahneman & Tversky 2000; Kahneman 2011).

The two schools of countervailing thought – Rational Choice Theory (Rationalists) versus Behavioral (Behavioralists) – represent two very different sides of the same academic coin. In simple terms, the debate can be framed as a clash between economists (advocating that rational choice exclusively dictates our decision-making apparatus) and humanists (advocating that behavioral-based human factors can and do influence, in part or whole, an individual's decision-making analysis in practice).

Which side is right – are individuals rational or not?

To get to the answer, the reader will now be subject to a series of 'what would you do?' choices based on hypothetical scenarios. The reader will then be asked to make a choice (as a general matter, assuming very little or no further information).

The pedagogical purpose of having the reader go through such hands-on decision-making exercises is several-fold. First, the reader's answers will provide one (very personal and thus vivid) "data point" as to a possible answer (on the reader's own "personal answer curve"). Second, the interactive nature of invoking a participatory reader approach will make the learning process and takeaways that much more poignant, and thus, more effective and enduring.

Now, for the series of short questions that follow, you will be asked to choose one of the two possible provided options. In choosing, you should not be concerned about making the "right" choice, but rather, should instead focus on making an honest (true) answer without the cognitive clutter of overanalysis. Moreover, the reader should opt for the answer that would "actually" be chosen (in the real world) rather than choosing an answer that the reader believe "should" or "ought" to be chosen (in concept or theory).

Of the following questions, choose one of the two options only (A or B). In doing so, the reader should also contemplate not just "what" choice to make, but also "why" such choice was selected.

Experiential exercises

1. A lotto ticket is given with the following two options:

    Choice A: Win $100 (guaranteed)
    Choice B: Win a 90 percent chance of winning $120

    Answer (A or B): _____

2. A lotto ticket is given with the following two options:

    Choice A: Win $1,000 (guaranteed)
    Choice B: Win a 90 percent chance of winning $1,200

    Answer (A or B): _____

3. A city fine (parking ticket) must be paid with the following two options:

    Choice A: Pay the fine of $100 (for sure)
    Choice B: Pay the fine based on a 10 percent chance of paying $0, and
    a 90 percent chance of paying $120

    Answer (A or B): _____

4. A city fine (parking ticket) must be paid with the following two options:

    Choice A: Pay $1,000 (for sure)
    Choice B: Pay based on a 10 percent chance of paying $0, and a 90
    percent chance of paying $1,200

    Answer (A or B): _____

Following are several more hands-on, experiential exercises:

5. Suppose A (the reader) is now at a trendy and popular fast fashion clothing store. A sees a t-shirt that A adores for $10. However, A then discovers that at a nearby (similarly trendy and popular) clothing store, the same t-shirt sells for $5 (half the price). However, the other clothing store is a 15-minute walk from the current store. Would A (the reader) walk 15 minutes to buy the same t-shirt at half-price?

    Answer (Yes or No): _____
    Why?

6. Suppose A (the reader, again) goes shopping for a new smartphone. A sees a smartphone model A likes very much for $500. However, A then discovers that a nearby store that is 15 minutes away sells the exact same smartphone (model, color, specifications) for $5 less. Would you walk 15 minutes to save 1 percent?

    Answer (Yes or No): _____
    Why?

For Questions 7 and 8, consider that you are faced with a life-impacting medical decision. Your physician informs you of a serious and sudden medical condition that is readily apparent based on a recent medical exam. Your physician recommends surgery to mitigate or cure the medical condition. However, you are then told that a "10 percent death rate" for the recommended surgery exists. The physician goes on to say, "What this means is that one out of ten people dies during surgery." The alternative is radiation treatment, with little research or data that exist pertaining to it, except that a roughly 50/50 chance exists of mitigating or curing the illness.

7. Which medical option should you choose, and why?

    A. Surgery
    B. Non-surgery (radiation)

    Answer (Yes or No): _____
    Why?

In the next scenario the same facts apply, except that your physician informs you that the recommended surgery has a "90 percent *survival* rate"; the physician further states that "What this means is that nine out of ten people come out of the surgery successfully." The alternative is the same as before, which is radiation treatment, with little research or data that exist pertaining to it, except that a roughly 50/50 chance exists of mitigating or curing the illness.

8.   Which medical option should you choose, and why?

A. Surgery
B. Non-surgery (radiation)

Answer (Yes or No): _____
Why?

Please write all the reader's answers here:

1.   _____

2.   _____

3.   _____

4.   _____

5.   _____

6.   _____

7.   _____

8.   _____

Now is a good time to review the foregoing experiential exercises, before the questions and scenarios are analyzed below. As a reminder, this analysis is done to answer the threshold question of whether, in a persuasion context, actors always make "rational" choices pursuant to RCT.

Decision analysis: Each of the foregoing scenarios has been restated in the next section, along with the relevant analysis.

This then leads to the question: What type of "rational analysis" should, in theory, be used to analyze the cases seen in these scenarios?

Expected value

The use of Expected Value (EV) is a fundamental tool that reflects rational analysis. EV, per its descriptive term, is an anticipated value for a given, expected future payout factoring in infinite iterations (Hamming 1991; Ross 2007).

As a simple example, the EV of flipping a two-sided coin and getting heads (rather than tails) is 50 percent. Such forecast is based on the coin being flipped an infinite number of times. This does not mean, however, that heads will be the outcome exactly once every two times the coin is flipped. The reason is because the expected outcome is not always the actual outcome, particularly in the short term, since such expected value is based on a long-term scenario analysis (to a time series from one to infinity). However, as a coin is flipped more and more times (with more transactions/event iterations), a greater convergence and accuracy of the EV calculation generally exists (adhering to a phenomenon known as the Law of Large Numbers, or LLN).

In the United States, for instance, there is a coin toss just prior to the beginning of the Super Bowl football championship game (one of American's most-watched yearly television events). This coin toss is an important feature of the game because the outcome determines which of the two competing teams will have the first option to play on offense or defense initially. Of the past 50 Super Bowl games, the EV calculus would predict that of the 50 coin flips, the coin would land on "heads" 25 times, and on "tails" the remaining 25 times. This is the theoretical calculation. But what exactly are the actual results in practice? Does the theory underlying EV clash or conform to what occurred – in the real (sports) world?

Of the 50 Super Bowl championship game coin tosses, the coin has landed on heads 24 times, and landed on tails 26 times. While 24 out of 50 is admittedly not exactly 50 percent, still, it is very close. And one could argue that additional flips of the coin would get the percentage to increasingly converge closer to 50 percent (Knudson 2016).

Parsing through the data, it is imperative not to be "fooled by randomness" (an expression from Nassim Nicholas Taleb) (Taleb 2005). For instance, as of this writing, the last four Super Bowl coin tosses have landed on tails four consecutive times, whereas the previous five times have landed on tails.

Returning to the original question, applying EV explains "why" Choice B is the apparent "rational" choice.

1.   *A lotto ticket is given with the following two options:*

     Choice A: Win $100 (guaranteed)
     Choice B: Win a 90 percent chance of winning $120

The "rational" choice is B. The "right" choice, however, may arguably be more subjective based on a particular person's tastes and preferences (including risk preferences). But if one believes or wants to believe that actors should make decisions on a rational basis pursuant to RCT, then using "rational behavior" and thus rational analysis should be the method by which to choose an answer – specifically, by using EV.

Applying Expected Value can be done by using the following formula:

Expected Value (EV) = Amount × Probability of Occurrence

Therefore:

Choice A:

Step 1: EV = $100 × 100%
Step 2: EV = $100 × 1.0
Step 3: EV = $100

Compared with:

Choice B:

Step 1: EV = $120 × 90%
Step 2: EV = $120 × 0.9
Step 3: EV = $108

Comparing Choice A versus Choice B

EV (Choice A) = $100
EV (Choice B) = $108

Therefore:

$108 (Choice B) > $100 (Choice A)

Therefore:

Choice: B

Underlying assumption:

Rational behavior

To test whether rational behavior held true en masse, the foregoing question was posed to participants in a large research survey. The expectation, under the purview of RCT, is that the majority of participants should choose Choice B. However, in practice (in the real world), the majority of participants opted not for Choice B, but for Choice A. That is, many participants failed to act rationally in its traditional sense (Kahneman, Slovic & Tversky 1982).

Why then did many participants fail to make the rational choice?

The main rationale in the study given for answering Choice B – the presumptively non-rational choice – was the need for financial safety and security. The wording, or similarly used wording of "guaranteed" or "for sure" made many participants "risk averse." In other words, such participants opted for getting fewer returns in exchange for less risk (specifically in this case, zero risk for the guaranteed monetary amount). For many in the study, such trade-off was worthwhile and made sense. But the wrinkle is that such decision-making process and decision outcome do not fully comport to rational decision-making behavior.

To explain such seemingly non-rational choices, the argument could be made that the survey's outcome merely reflected different risk preferences and profiles. However, the representative sample used in the widely cited survey (often a bellwether standard for statistical analysis) would have "flattened" (lowered) the existence and disposition of risk preferences at the macro level given the large representative sample size.

The reader may now use this opportunity to reflect upon the decision made for the foregoing scenario. Was Choice A or B chosen, and why? Again, not one "right" answer exists per se, which is precisely one take-away from this experiential exercise. People are people. Given this, different factors – some rational, some outside the rational zone – may take dominant control of a person's decision-making process within a persuasion context. Arguably, this is not because a person is ill-informed, but rather, it is that other humanistic factors may play a role as part of the human condition and psyche.

2. *A lotto ticket is given with the following two options:*

    Choice A: Win $1,000 (guaranteed)
    Choice B: Win a 90 percent chance of winning $1,200

The "rational" choice is B (again). The same EV calculus can be applied to this question as in the first question.

As the reader may have noted, the second question was seemingly similar to Question 1. One key difference is that the dollar amounts were changed from $100 to $1,000 for Choice A, and from $120 to $1,200 for Choice B.

Why was this change (adding a zero to each number) done? Should such change lead to any significant decision-making outcomes, according to RCT?

In short, the dollar amount changes were done to "stress-test" whether the reader's underlying principles remained the same (stayed constant). Rational behavior would generally dictate that the exact same EV calculation should again be used, and that the increase in relevant commensurate amounts, even in multiplicity, should not make a material difference in terms of rational behavior analysis and decision-making – at least in theory.

Thus, applying the same EV formula:

Expected Value (EV) = Amount × Probability of Occurrence

Therefore:

Choice A:

Step 1: EV = $1,000 × 100%
Step 2: EV = $1,000 × 1.0
Step 3: EV = $1,000

Compared with:

Choice B:

Step 1: EV = $1,200 × 90%
Step 2: EV = $1,200 × 0.9
Step 3: EV = $1,080

Comparing Choice A versus Choice B

EV (Choice A) = $1,000 (gain)
EV (Choice B) = $1,080 (gain)

Therefore:

$1,080 (Choice B) > $1,000 (Choice A)

Therefore:

Choice B

Underlying Assumption:

Rational Behavior

The foregoing approach again strives to answer the question of: What is the "rational" choice? This is again separate and distinguishable from what may be the "right" choice for any given individual, as discussed previously.

This leads to the next question, raised earlier, of whether such dollar amount change is significant or not. The argument can be made that change in a given amount should allow for a change in options. Here, the changing of the dollar amount increased the relevant amount by tenfold. Thus, under this lens, with ten times the amount of money can come a different calculus.

However, underlying rational behavior – which underlies the EV calculus – the exact same "logic" and reasoning should stay constant regardless of whether the number shifted from 10 to 100, or 1,000 to 1 million. Here, as before, EV should be used to make a rational decision.

3. *A city fine (parking ticket) must be paid with the following two options:*

> *Choice A: Pay $100 (for sure)*
> *Choice B: Pay based on a 10 percent chance of paying $0, and a 90*
> *   percent chance of paying $120*

As the reader has likely noticed, unlike Questions 1 and 2 that were framed in terms of gains, this question is framed in terms of losses. Should this make any difference?

Here, the "rational" choice is A. The reasoning is the same as with the previous two scenarios: the EV – framed in terms of negative value (since it involves paying a fine) – is better for Choice A than for Choice B.

The EV calculation is as follows:

Expected Value (EV) = Amount × Probability of Occurrence

Therefore:

Choice A:

> Step 1: EV = −$100 × 100%
> Step 2: EV = −$100 × 1.0
> Step 3: EV = −$100 (loss)

Compared with:

Choice B:

> Step 1: EV = −$120 × 90%
> Step 2: EV = −$120 × 0.9
> Step 3: EV = −$108

Comparing Choice A versus Choice B

EV (Choice A) = −$100 (loss)
EV (Choice B) = −$108 (loss)

Therefore (from a cost minimization purview):

−$100 (Choice A) < −$108 (Choice B)

Therefore:

Choice A

Underlying Assumption:

Rational Behavior

The survey data relating to this question showed an interesting participant pattern, a quasi-quirky tendency among some people. In this slightly tweaked version of the original question – framed negatively in terms of possible losses rather than possible gains – many of the participants shifted to Choice B (from Choice A in the original question) (Kahneman, Slovic & Tversky 1982).

Whereas in the original version of the question (again framed in terms of possible dollar amount gains), most of the participants wanted the "sure thing" or "guaranteed amount" in exchange for less risk, primarily linked to reasons related to financial safety and security. Thus, as rational actors, such thinking process should stay constant to be consistent with transitivity noted previously in this section.

However, counter to RCT, adherence to the transitivity principle failed to hold true for many people. The mere (inverse, negative) reframing of the elicited question compelled somewhat contradictory and arguably "irrational" behavior, in which many people shifted to choose B over A. Rather than stay true and consistent to the rationale of opting for a guaranteed outcome (result), many chose instead to trade (swap) a guaranteed loss with instead a possibly higher chance of paying more combined with a lower chance of not paying anything. This type of behavior is known as loss aversion theory (LAT).

Put simply, people became risk-takers with potential losses. And people became risk-avoiders with potential gains. But under RCT, the mere framing of the question should not make any material difference in decision-making. Yet in practice with real (rather than imagined) people involved, the framing of how a question is asked (half-full or half-empty glass perspective) led to discernible decision-making differences.

Such behavior – which some attribute to "irrational exuberance" or "animal spirits" – may, at least in part, explain the behavior of many gamblers from Las Vegas to Macau, and among colleagues and friends. At the broader level, since decision-making exists everywhere, such behavior may arguably also be seen among businesspeople in boardrooms and policy makers in various sectors.

When beginning to see the landscape (the gambler's specific casino table with other players) in terms of mounting gambling losses, it may in theory be the "rational choice" to quit the game to minimize losses. In contrast, many gamblers instead may opt to "double down" or "throw good money after bad money" by focusing on the relatively small and remote chance (low probability event) of getting back to zero (or even above zero). Statistically, such behavior and decision-making process will work against the gambler, while being beneficial to the house (casino) at the cost of the players (gamblers) in a zero-sum game since "the house always wins" (at least in the long-run).

4. *A city fine (parking ticket) must be paid with the following two options:*

Choice A: Pay $1,000 (for sure)
Choice B: Pay based on a 10 percent chance of paying $0, and a 90 percent chance of paying $1,200

The "rational" choice is again Choice A. Much like with Question 2 analyzed previously, the main material difference was adding a zero to all of the relevant dollar amounts. Everything else on paper remains the same. But the question is whether the analysis and decision-making process stays the same or differs for individuals.

In theory, as discussed previously, the change of paying $1,000 (instead of $100) and paying $1,200 (instead of $120) should be insignificant from a RCT purview. However, for those who did switch answers and rationales, it is likely that a deviation from rational behavior may have occurred. As with Question 3, the negative framing of the choices (in terms of possible losses) in Question 4 led many people to shift from Choice A ("for sure") to Choice B (10 percent chance of $0) for the arguably Behavioralist proclivity to seek survival by focusing on the (low probability) chance of escaping from negative territory back to par or positive territory.

Following is the relevant EV calculus:

Expected Value (EV) = Amount × Probability of Occurrence

Therefore:

Choice A:

Step 1: EV = −$1,000 × 100%
Step 2: EV = −$1,000 × 1.0
Step 3: EV = −$1,000

Compared with:

Choice B:

Step 1: EV = −$1,200 × 90%
Step 2: EV = −$1,200 × 0.9
Step 3: EV = −$1,080

Comparing Choice A versus Choice B

EV (Choice A) = −$1,000 (loss)
EV (Choice B) = −$1,080 (loss)

Therefore:

−$1,000 (Choice A) < −$1,080 (Choice B)

Therefore:

Choice A

Underlying Assumption:

Rational Behavior

5. *Suppose A (the reader) is now at a trendy and popular fast fashion cloth-ing store. A sees a t-shirt that A adores for $10. However, A then discov-ers that at a nearby (similarly trendy and popular) clothing store, the same t-shirt sells for $5 (half the price). However, the other clothing store is a 15-minute walk from the current store. Would A (the reader) walk 15 minutes to buy the same t-shirt at half-price (to save $5)?*

The main takeaway from this question, as with all the questions in this section, is not to test a per se right or wrong answer. It is instead intended to mea-sure consistency (transitivity) in decision-making. For those who did choose to walk 15 minutes to save $5, this might be derived from a cost-of-time (or opportunity cost) calculation. A 15-minute walk for $5 would equate to an earnings amount of $20 per hour. Depending on the subjective value of this objective calculation, some may decide that it is worthwhile to walk 15 min-utes to save $5, which in effect, would be saying that the individual would be satisfied making $20/hour (or alternatively, $5 for 15 minutes). Other factors may also be incorporated, such as an individual's chosen reference point for a similar task or T-shirt (for instance, the same individual may have the opportu-nity to earn no more than $20 per hour elsewhere).

Conversely, another individual using this same cost-of-time (opportunity cost) metric may instead decide that it is not worthwhile to walk 15 minutes to buy the same T-shirt for $5 cheaper. Depending on the individual, such decision could be based on the same analysis of the objective calculation based on other opportunities that could instead be pursued (whereby the individual could earn relatively more than $20/hour). No matter the deci-sion, the question would be framed as, "Is the 15-minute walk worth saving

$5?" For purposes of this experiential exercise, as before, no one answer is necessarily better than the other.

No matter what decision is made – to walk the 15 minutes to save $5, or not – this methodology of determining a decision outcome would generally be based on an absolute (not relative) basis in terms of total dollars earned or saved (rather than dollars earned or saved on a percentage basis, which is described further below).

Alternatively, a relative basis approach could be used. Under such relative basis approach, the individual would view taking the 15-minute walk as a means to save 50 percent off ($5 of $10) of the normal purchase price. In this case, the question would be framed as, "Is the 15-minute walk worth saving 50 percent?"

For some individuals, this is a decision game-changer. The decision to walk 15 minutes to another store to buy a T-shirt at half price would be worth the extra effort. The previously presented approach of framing the question in terms of cost-of-time (absolute basis) would be trumped by the relative basis approach of thinking of the 15-minute walk as a half-off proposition.

The reader should now recall, first, what answer, and second, what approach – relative or absolute basis – was used in getting to an answer and rationale for such answer. This will be helpful for the following analysis as well.

6. *Suppose A (the reader) goes shopping for a new smartphone. Person A sees a smartphone model that A likes very much for $500. However, A then discovers that a nearby store that is 15 minutes away sells the exact same smartphone (model, color, specifications) for $5 less. Would A walk 15 minutes to save 1% ($5 of $500)?*

This hypothetical scenario is both similar and dissimilar to Question 5. One similarity is that the opportunity to save $5 for a 15-minute walk to a nearby store for the same good exists here as in the T-shirt example. One difference, however, is that the price of the good itself, here a smartphone, has been changed to $500 (rather than $10 in the previous case). Should this make a decision-making difference, rationally speaking?

This depends on whether an absolute or relative basis approach is used to frame the question. The results of the two approaches, as the reader may have noted already, tends to yield dramatically different results.

If the cost-of-time (absolute) basis approach is used, then this will lead to the same $20-per-hour calculation as in the earlier t-shirt example. Similarly, the availability of other opportunity costs and/or reference points will be used as tools, reference points, and benchmarks to help guide the individual toward a decision based on such rationale.

If instead a relative basis approach is used, a more dramatic forecasted future yield differential will result. With the original T-shirt question, a 50 percent price reduction would be the value received of walking 15 minutes for the same T-shirt in a different store. But here, the calculation applied to the smartphone question would instead only yield a mere 1 percent discount for taking the 15-minute walk. Note that no matter how the overall price of the items change, the issue remains the same of whether to walk 15 minutes to save $5.

Bearing this in mind, the question of whether individuals act rationally can be reconsidered.

If an individual was "presumed rational," then the absolute approach of using a cost-of-time approach would compel the individual to choose the same outcome for both the smartphone case as the T-shirt case. After all, the individual is saving the exact same amount of money on a time basis – $20 per hour. The mere fact that the amount in question is $5 less of $10, $5 less of $500, or $5 less of any other figure, should be largely immaterial and irrelevant. What would also be considered largely immaterial and irrelevant is the percentage-basis savings under RCT. The 50 percent discount in the T-shirt example compared with the 1 percent discount in the smartphone example would generally be, from a Rationalist's perspective, a non-factor in the calculus. In other words, the contextual issue of whether $5 is saved of $10 (T-shirt) or $500 (smartphone) should largely serve as immaterial background noise, according to Rationalists.

Now the reader can think back to the answers and rationale in this and the former questions. What basis was used – absolute or relative? Was the same methodology used for both cases? Why or why not? Reflecting on these points will help provide one more data point in terms of whether rational behavior was used or not – and if not, whether constant conformity to rational behavior is necessarily a good or bad process and outcome, both in theory and in the real world.

But what about the subjective perceptional difference between the two examples? As discussed previously in this book, framing and perception is a derivative of psychological influence and other hidden forces, not a dispassionate calculus applied by Rationalists.

Continuing onward is the next question and related analysis:

> *Consider next that you are faced with a life-impacting decision. Your physician informs you of a serious and sudden medical condition that is readily apparent based on a recent medical exam. Your physician recommends surgery to mitigate or possibly cure the medical condition. However, you are then told that a "10 percent death rate" for the recommended surgery exists. The physician goes on to say, "What this means is that one out of ten people die during surgery." The alternative is radiation treatment, with little research or data that exist*

pertaining to it, except that a roughly 50/50 chance exists of mitigating or curing the illness.

7. *Which medical option should you choose, and why?*

   A. Surgery
   B. Non-surgery (radiation)

This scenario again is not necessarily to ascertain a right or wrong answer. Rather it is to determine what approach was used and the rationale applied to get to an answer.

Applying the Expected Value (EV) approach:

A: EV = 1 × 0.1 = 10% (death rate)
B: EV = 1 × 0.5 = 50% (death rate)

From a Rationalist's purview, the "right" (logical and rational) option would be Option A. Option A, elective surgery, after all, has a lower death/mortality rate of 10 percent (compared with 50 percent for Option B, radiation therapy).

This seems fairly straightforward. So what is the issue?

The issue arises when the methodology used in this example is compared with the methodology used in the next similar but distinguishable decision:

> *The next scenario is the same as the prior situation, except that your physician informs you that the recommended surgery has a "90 percent survival rate," further stating that, "What this means is that nine out of ten people come out of the surgery successfully." The alternative is the same as before, which is radiation treatment, with little research or data that exists pertaining to it, except that a roughly 50/50 chance exists of mitigating or curing the illness.*

8. *Which medical option should A choose, and why?*

   A. Surgery
   B. Non-surgery (radiation)

This example is substantially similar to the prior example, but with one notable difference: The wording was changed from "10 percent *death* rate" (framed as a loss) to "90 percent *survival* rate" (framed as a gain). Are these simply two immaterial sides of the same proverbial coin – or a material decision-making difference? Apart from whether a difference exists, *should* this change have made a difference, rationally speaking?

To begin the same methodological analysis, an Expectation Value (EV) calculation yields the exact same results in this "survival rate" version as with the earlier "death rate" version.

A: $EV = 1 \times 0.9 = 90\%$ (survival rate)
B: $EV = 1 \times 0.5 = 50\%$ (survival rate)

Under RCT, since the exact same EV results exist for both scenarios, no differences exist between the two choices under this purview. Both EV yields for each of the two cases, A and B, are exactly the same.

Under the Behavioralist approach, however, a notable difference may exist separate from the EV yields. With Question 7, the framing of the question was in terms of losses, specifically in terms of death (mortality). But the very next question was framed in terms of gains, specifically in terms of survival (success). Rationalists would adamantly argue that the mere framing effect of a question is immaterial and irrelevant. After all, a mere framing effect should not impact the substantive calculus, with the difference in diction only representing superficial dressing akin to "half empty" versus "half full."

Now is a good time for the reader to revisit the choice made for this question along with the rationale given for it. If the same EV calculation was used for both scenarios, pursuant to transitivity, then this would generally conform to rational choice theory.

The reader may now be curious as to how other individuals decided. After all, if other people acted consistently in using an EV calculus to determine what decision to make, then this would provide a useful data point as well in terms of answering the question of whether individuals (at large) are Rationalists or Behavioralists. If all people were fully rational, people's answers should not vary based on how the question was framed.

To this point, a large survey was conducted relating to these scenarios. When framed negatively in terms of death rates (framed as losses), only 54 percent chose elective surgery. When framed positively in terms of survival rates (framed as gains), the number jumped by more than half to 82 percent who chose elective surgery. Other studies have affirmed the framing effect (Almashat, Ayotte, Edelstein & Margrett 2008). Again this view clashes with Rationalists, who would adamantly argue that no difference should exist because of a mere framing effect.

Now consider the public policy ramifications of how persuasion can occur through word choice and the framing effect. As a result of how a question is asked – a hidden force in persuasion – the expected outcome in terms of people opting for elective surgery decisions varied dramatically: 54 percent compared with 82 percent. Thus, as a general matter, many people were not entirely consistent with rational behavior and decision-making.

Does this make individuals bad or uninformed? This is debatable and the space constraints of this book do not adequately allow for a full spectrum of viewpoints.

Perhaps, though, it can suffice for now to merely say this: As social animals (*Homo sapiens* are biologically animal primates who share at least a 90 percent DNA similarity with our next closest biological relatives, chimpanzees), an instant-response operating system exists to make rapid-fire "fight or flight" responses. (Think: walking alone in a secluded, dark forest when a bear suddenly appears out of nowhere.)

Under such environment, having the luxury of time to conduct an expected value analysis would not exist. Only very recently, under modern conditions complete with steel-framed buildings, air-conditioned offices, sophisticated computing technology, and secure surroundings does the opportunity for such constant and methodical Rationalist analysis exist. This is a somewhat layered way of saying that, according to this argument, both the Rationalist and Behavioralist schools of thought could co-exist within decision-making contexts.

A central theme of this chapter is whether rational behavior that "ought" to occur in theory "actually" does occur in the real world. Or are we subject to mental shortcuts (hidden heuristics) as also described in this book? This chapter provides examples and evidence into these fundamental questions. Bearing this in mind, it may also be useful to note Albert Einstein's famous quote: "In theory, theory and practice are the same. In practice, they are not."

Case

Multinational businesses are often presumed to act rationally in the pursuit of "maximizing shareholder value." The ability to increase share prices by increasing revenue and/or minimizing costs is of particular and paramount corporate concern. The failure to exercise this duty could lead to tangible ramifications. A corporation's board of directors may, for instance, elect to fire and replace the CEO and/or other C-level executives. Exacerbating such pressure for profit is the risk of potential litigation, especially among technology firms highly protective of their intellectual property (IP) rights. This has led to the potential of massive losses that could negatively affect a firm's bottom line.

In the smartphone space, two of the largest tech titans are Apple (based in Cupertino, California) and Samsung (based in Seoul, South Korea). The two titans fluctuate between cooperation and non-cooperation, depending on the transactions in play. But as Samsung's smartphone market share began to rise in recent years, threatening Apple's market position, another dimension in the business competition chess game emerged in the form of a lawsuit by Apple against Samsung for alleged IP infringement. After several rounds of out-of-court, pre-trial negotiation attempts, a formal lawsuit was filed by Apple against Samsung. Many in Silicon Valley and beyond waited with bated breath for the court's verdict because of its potential ripple effects in the tech space.

As noted by the Program on Negotiation at Harvard Law School, in August 2012 a California jury ruled that Samsung should pay Apple more than $1 billion in damages for patent violations of Apple products, particularly Apple's iPhone. The judge subsequently reduced the amount to $600 million. In November 2013, another jury ruled that Samsung should pay Apple $290 million of the amount overruled by the judge in the earlier 2012 case.

In negotiations between Apple and Samsung, Apple argued that it had lost significant profits in the smartphone market as a result of, among other things, Samsung's allegedly copied features of the iPhone. Samsung counter-argued that its consumers purchased Samsung smartphones for other reasons, such as Samsung's bigger screens and cheaper price points, according to the *The New York Times*. Both Apple and Samsung decided against an out-of-court settlement, and instead, opted for in-court litigation involving highly paid attorneys and intense media scrutiny.

(Because many of the negotiation details are not disclosed and publicly available, some assumptions for pedagogical purposes are made here.)

From Apple's perspective, based on academic assumptions made for this case, its expectation value (EV) calculation may have been that it (Apple) could successfully sue for $2 billion, of which, Apple in its internal calculation would take the view that a court would award $2 billion to Apple three out of every four times. It is often the case that plaintiffs (Apple in this particular case) have been shown to be relatively optimistic (confident or even overconfident) about the chance of a verdict in their favor.

Apple could further take the view that an out-of-court negotiated settlement with Samsung would yield a much lower figure than what it would receive as plaintiffs in an in-court lawsuit. Specifically, Apple might take the view that Samsung would offer $500 million four out of every five times.

Thus, Apple's EV calculation would be the following:

Option A (litigation): EV = $2 billion × 0.75 = $1.5 billion

versus

Option B (out-of-court settlement): EV = $500 million × 0.8 = $400 million

If acting rationally, and pursuant to RCT, Apple should choose Option A for litigation (EV = $1.5 billion) and reject Samsung's negotiated offer (EV = $400 million) since Option A's EV was greater than Option B's EV by a notable amount, nearly 400 percent more ($1.5 billion versus $400 million).

From Samsung's perspective, after consulting internally (among its board and officers) and externally (with outside legal counsel, consultants, and other parties), Samsung may take the view that its litigation risk is fairly remote since it believes that no blatant copying of IP rights occurred as Apple alleged. As such, Samsung may then take the view that a 25 percent chance existed that a court would award Apple $400 million. Samsung may have also assumed that a relatively smaller amount of $200 million would be offered by Apple in an out-of-court settlement, with an estimated 75 percent likelihood of occurrence.

Thus, Samsung's EV calculation would be the following:

Option A (litigation): EV = $400 million × 0.25 = −$100 million

versus

Option B (out-of-court settlement): EV = $200 million × 0.75 = −$150 million

If acting rationally, and pursuant to RCT, Samsung should choose Option A for litigation (EV = −$100 million) and reject an anticipated negotiated offer with Apple (EV = −$150 million) since Option A's EV loss was greater than Option B's EV loss by a notable amount (paying $150 million versus paying $100 million, a difference of $50 million).

Clearly, the EV calculations by Apple and Samsung differ greatly (based on the hypothetical nature of the numbers in this case study). This is not entirely unusual in the real world. However, since both plaintiffs and defendants can often overestimate each of their respective probabilities for success, such factors can also explain why out-of-court negotiations can fail. It is such disparate gaps in the parties' EV calculus that can often lead to costly and extensive litigation. This is good news for lawyers (framed as revenue gains), but perhaps not so good news for certain businesses (framed as litigation losses).

Bibliography

Almashat, S, Ayotte, B, Edelstein, B, & Margrett, J 2008, 'Framing Effect Debiasing in Medical Decision Making', *Patient Education and Counseling*, vol. 71, no. 1, pp. 102–107. Available from: Elsevier, Amsterdam. [8 January 2018].

Arrow, K 1951, *Social Choice and Individual Values*, Yale University Press, New Haven.

Hamming, RW 1991, *The Art of Probability: For Scientist and Engineers*, Addison-Wesley, Boston.

Kahneman, D 2011, *Thinking, Fast and Slow*, Farrar, Straus and Giroux, New York.

Kahneman, D, Diener, E, & Schwarz, N 1999, *Well-Being: The Foundations of Hedonic Psychology*, Russell Sage Foundation, New York.

Kahneman, D, Slovic, P, & Tversky, A 1982, *Judgement under Uncertainty: Heuristics and Biases*, Cambridge University Press, Cambridge. Available from: https://philpapers.org/rec/KAHJUU. [18 December 2018].

Kahneman, D, & Tversky, A 2000, *Choices, Values and Frames*, Cambridge University Press, Cambridge.

Knudson, K 2016, *The Predictive Power of the Super Bowl Coin Toss*. Available from: www.forbes.com/sites/kevinknudson/2016/02/04/the-predictive-power-of-the-super-bowl-coin-toss/#3fb155446beb. [8 January 2018].

Regenwetter, M, Dana, J, & Davis-Stober, CP 2011, 'Transitivity of Preferences', *Psychology Review*. Available from: www.ncbi.nlm.nih.gov/pubmed/21244185. [11 November 2017].

Ross, SM 2007, *Introduction to Probability Models*, Academic Press, Amsterdam.

Taleb, NN 2005, *Fooled by Randomness: The Hidden Role of Chance in Life and in the Markets*, Random House, New York.

7 Elements

Creative ways to supersize the pie

Negotiation

Negotiation is defined as a "communication process that helps resolve disputes and plan transactions" (Wiggins & Lowry 2005). Negotiation is a process by which disputes can be resolved and value can be created for the parties involved. The formality of negotiations can vary greatly – from a formal negotiation setting in a conference room meeting to email exchanges between parties thousands of miles apart – regarding terms and conditions of a particular agreement.

Within the given definition for negotiation exists two distinct types of negotiations. The "'resolve disputes" wording of the negotiation definition refers to a concept known as a dispute settlement negotiation (DSN). A dispute settlement negotiation is a negotiation that is primarily backward-looking (historically focused) rather than forward-looking (future-focused). That is, a DSN is typically where the negotiation parties meet to resolve or litigate a dispute that occurred in the past. The general expectation in a DSN is for the aggrieved party to receive what was perceived to have been lost (and be put back to par). A typical DSN example is litigation between two disputing parties in court (Sander & Rubin 1988).

The "plan transactions" wording of the negotiation definition refers to a concept known as a deal-making negotiation (DMN). A DMN – in contrast to a DSN – is a negotiation that is primarily forward-looking (future-focused) rather than backward-looking (historically focused). That is, a DMN is one in which the negotiation parties are seeking ways to cooperate now and in the future, so that both parties would potentially be better off working together than apart (Sander & Rubin 1988). A typical DMN example is a joint venture (JV) between two companies that potentially benefits both sides.

At a more conceptual level, two main schools of thought exist relating to negotiations, both generally predicated on rational behavior: (1) positional (distributive) bargaining (red zone bargaining style), and (2) principled (integrative) bargaining models (blue zone bargaining style). A "mixed motive" negotiation involves aspects of both positional and principled bargaining models.

Bargaining models

Positional bargaining (also referred to as distributive bargaining) exists when negotiating parties focus primarily on their own individual (self-focused) positions. Examples of positions include price, quantity, land area, and time. Typically, positional bargaining occurs with little or no exploration of the other side's interests (defined as the rationale underlying one's position). Positional bargaining is often equated to "competitive" and "hard" negotiations in which a clear "winner" or "loser" is expected. Other working assumptions underlying the positional (distributive) bargaining model include a fixed pie, competitive mind-set, DSN-based outcomes, and a zero-sum game. As such, under the distributive bargaining model, the typical dominant strategy would be not to cooperate fully, but rather, to try to "win" or "get as much" substance (utility or benefit) from the other side as possible. However, such pursuit often comes at the cost of a suboptimal or damaged relationship. Here, hidden assumptions underlying this style of negotiation behavior often serves as impasses toward building trust, and can be akin to World War I–era trench warfare, in which each side draws a line in the sand signaling clear positions that must be defended by the parties. The distributive bargaining model can thus incentivize the following negotiation tactics: extreme offers, hard haggling, and unethical behavior (in which puffery related to set positions borders on and often enters into deceptive and unethical behavior).

What is an example of the positional bargaining model in the real world? One may see positional bargaining at work in many instances in life, such as at a weekend flea market for a used coffee table. In this example, the bargaining exchange may begin with the buyer offering the seller, say, $50 (the buyer's first offer) for the coffee table, to which the seller can make a very quick counteroffer of, say, $100 (the seller's counteroffer). Then what follows is what is known as the "negotiation dance," in which both sides, if interested, typically begin making concessions, often toward a price point somewhere near the middle point of both beginning offers, say, at $75, for the coffee table.

Because the negotiators assume a fixed pie (or zero-sum game) – a hidden force in negotiations – the negotiators are in effect engaged in a "land grab" whereby one party's gain is directly assumed to be correlated to the counterparty's loss – not too dissimilar to a game of football or similar win-lose sporting competition. Thus, the more "points" (in the form of price, quantity, land area, time, etc.) gained from the other side, the better it is from a positional negotiator's perspective, since the goal of positional bargaining is to gain (win) as much as possible.

In contrast, principled (or integrative) bargaining involves a different approach – not to negotiate "against" the counterparty, but instead, to negotiate "with" the counterparty (using a mental model of "we" rather than "us versus them"). In other words, by linking or integrating both sides, opportunities may arise that could potentially add value for each party. Working assumptions underlying principled (integrative) bargaining include: expanding the pie, a cooperative mindset, and a DMN-driven "win-win" (rather than "win-lose") positive-sum game (playing field). One of the main academic architects of integrative bargaining is derived from the book *Getting to Yes* by Roger Fisher and William Ury of Harvard University (Fisher & Ury 2011). The authors suggest a "seven elements" structured framework by which to conduct integrative bargaining, which often assumes rational behavior:

- Communication (building effective and respectful communication)
- Relationship (to understand and analyze the type of relationship sought)
- Interests (exploring common and shared interests underlying the parties' positions)
- Options (creating and brainstorming options with the counterparty)
- Legitimacy (seeking mutually agreeable objective standards)
- Alternatives (saying "no" to an offer because the offer by the counterparty is not better than one's "BATNA," the best alternative to a negotiated agreement; in essence, the highest opportunity cost or best walkaway alternative)
- Commitment (saying "yes" to an offer since it is better than one's BATNA)

The following section examines each of the seven elements in greater detail.

Communication involves both verbal and non-verbal communication. Studies suggest that non-verbal communication – facial expressions, body language, and tonality – constitute the dominant part of total communication. A widely cited study found that non-verbal communication played a particularly important role, whereby body language accounted for 55 percent of total communication (Mehrabian 2017). Thus, even if a party is not verbally articulating a point – or even remains predominantly silent or quiet in a negotiation setting – this does not always mean that such person is not communicating. In other words, one can communicate, and often does communicate, without words. From a persuasion perspective, the strategic issue becomes not whether to communicate, but how to effectively communicate to best achieve one's goal.

In contrast to the principled (integrative) bargaining model, from the purview of the positional (distributive) bargaining model, communication generally is viewed as relatively less important. Instead, communication is mostly done in an effort to signal or achieve dominance over the counterparty. Such dominance signals can come in many forms, including power, money, influence, and physical/intellectual superiority. In contrast, from the purview of the principled (integrative) bargaining model, communication generally is viewed as relatively more important. This is because effective communication is seen as having a greater likelihood of leading to a better relationship. Under the principled (integrative) bargaining model, effective communication and strong relationships have a positive correlation.

Relationships are a function of effective communication methods. As a default, most agree that good relationships are better than bad relationships, everything else being equal. But this is not the dispositive issue. The more dispositive issue is instead: What is a negotiation party willing to give in exchange for a better relationship? (Salacuse 2017).

This issue then leads to the need for a *relationship calculus*. Here, a party must determine the aspirational future relationship value for a particular counterparty (relative to the current future value for the same counterparty) based on the party's particular set of factors or success metrics. For simplicity of analysis, one can categorically assign one of three relationship values: high, medium, or low (a form of scenario analysis). The higher the aspirational future relationship value, for whatever reason as determined by the relevant party, the more strategic the party's communication strategy must be (Subramanian 2018). Conversely, the lower the aspirational future relationship value, for whatever reason as determined by the relevant party, the less strategic the party's communication strategy must be.

The next three elements – interests, options, and legitimacy – are referred to as the "circle of value" (Lax & Sebenius 2006). The "circle of value" terminology is used as symbolic reference to a pie that can potentially be increased in size – sometimes substantially (supersized) – if the elements are applied optimally in a negotiation context.

Interests reflect the (often unstated and unseen) concerns and desires of the negotiation parties. Put simply, interests are "why" a particular party wants a particular position (Shonk 2017). A position is "what" a particular party wants in a negotiation setting. Often, but not always, an interest is a narrative (rationale using words) for why a particular party wants or demands a particular position. Thus, an interest is generally qualitative in nature, whereas a position can often be quantified (by using numbers). For example, a banker's demand for a year-end bonus of $100,000 is the banker's (quantitative) position, while the banker's desire for greater wealth accumulation, status, and power may represent the banker's (qualitative) interests underlying the position.

Three types of interests exist: shared, complementary, and conflicting. A *shared interest* is an interest that all parties in a negotiation have in common. A *complementary interest* is an interest that differs among the parties but may have potential added value. A *conflicting interest* is an interest that differs among the parties, without any added value potential (Shonk 2017). The strategic framework underlying the principled (integrative) bargaining model is, first, to explore interests with the counterparty; second, categorize such interests together into shared, complementary, and conflicting interests; and third, find creative solutions through collaborative brainstorming based on such shared and complementary interests within the "circle of value" in an effort to "get to yes."

Options are potential creative solutions based on the shared and complementary interests of the relevant parties. To maximize options through collaborative brainstorming, several strategies exist. The first strategy is a "one-text" approach, in which the relevant parties share a common writing medium to write down ideas and options to signal a "one-text, one-team" mindset (in contrast to an "us versus them" mindset underlying the distributive bargaining model). The second strategy is to apply a "no-names basis" approach when brainstorming ideas and potential solutions (Fisher & Ury 2011). This is suggested as a means to create positive collaborative momentum, but also to minimize the potential of misunderstanding if and when a party's suggested option is later not chosen.

Legitimacy is then used to create an objective standard by which to choose one option (out of the potentially many options brainstormed in the previous step by the parties). Another term for legitimacy may be mutually agreeable objective standards. Examples include fair market value (FMV) for a particular good or service, the rule of law, customs, the opinion of a group of elders/scholars, and community/societal norms, to name just a few. Applying and overlaying such criteria to the collaboratively created options often helps to get from many options to one (best) option. Such best option represents the final agreed outcome in the negotiation.

Next, in the final (rational) calculus, the parties (individually and collectively) must then decide whether to say "yes" or "no" to the final offer from the negotiation process.

To do this, the parties must weigh (compare) the best option against their (best) *alternative*. Specifically, the party must weigh the negotiated offer (best option) with its BATNA (best alternative to a negotiated agreement). BATNA is a party's best walkaway alternative (or opportunity cost, using economics parlance) to the final negotiated offer (Fisher & Ury 2011).

Under the BATNA calculus, the parties should do the following (assuming rational behavior):

- If a party's BATNA is greater than an offer, then the party should choose its BATNA (say "no" to the counterparty)
- If a party's BATNA is less than an offer, then the party should choose its offer (say "yes" to the counterparty)

The final element of the seven elements framework is *commitment*. Commitment typically occurs when a party calculates that its BATNA is less than the negotiated best offer (assuming the offer and BATNA are not "on a par" and thus can be compared) (Chang 2017). Put simply, it is where the parties were able to "get to yes." Two types of commitment generally exist: non-verbal and verbal. A verbal commitment generally precedes any written commitment, and runs a greater risk of potential future misunderstanding among the parties. Given this, a non-verbal commitment may be most beneficial in a relatively high-trust negotiation environment, in which the parties know and trust each other based on past dealings or other circumstances. Outside such high-trust negotiation environments, a written commitment, often in the form of a legally binding agreement (contract) or treaty, may be a more strategic and sustainable form of commitment because written agreements more clearly evidence what the parties agreed upon for current and future reference. This then mitigates the risk of future misunderstanding and conflict.

Under the principled (integrative) negotiation model, the objective is to explore (rather than dictate) each parties' "interests" underneath a party's "position." This is often done by simply asking a very simple question: "Why?" (rather than "What?").

To apply this method to the previous coffee table purchase example, the buyer may want to ask why the seller wants a certain amount for the table. It could be that there is an underlying reason to rationalize the price (high quality of wood or craftsmanship, historical significance, etc.). This "why" interest-based approach can also be used by the buyer (a student with little cash who just wants basic cheap furniture for her dorm room, etc.). The underlying rationale is that exploring each party's underlying interests can help to bridge the gap between differences in a negotiation and persuasion context.

One advantage of the positional (distributive) bargaining model is that it is relatively fast since only the parties' positions need to be focused on, and further, that identifying the positions (price, quantity, time) of the related parties is often done relatively easily. One risk of such positional model, however, is that a win-lose, winner-takes-all positional bargaining approach may risk ruining the relationship since only the parties' positions are the main point of contention. Thus, the negotiation can at times lead to "negotiator's remorse" in which either or both sides are left with some form of regret or dissatisfaction following the conclusion of the negotiation – even after "getting to yes." Here, neither party may feel satisfied even after agreement, nor do they want to reopen negotiations if given the choice because of a lack of trust or good will unless absolutely compelled to do so. Given our current interconnected and globalized era, in which individuals exist within fewer and fewer degrees of separation, not forging strong relationships can often lead to inefficient and suboptimal negotiation outcomes in which the final negotiated solution makes neither side perfectly satisfied.

The advantage of the principled (integrative) bargaining model is that it focuses more on establishing stronger communication lines in an effort to forge a stronger relationship. Forging stronger relationships, in turn, generally fosters more creative brainstorming and option-building processes, which can then lead to more optimal negotiated outcomes. The risk of the principled (integrative) bargaining strategy is that, because it involves more elements and steps (exploring common interests, creating options together, seeking legitimate standards, and the like, per the seven elements approach), it often takes longer to reach a negotiated outcome compared with the more straightforward and simplistic positional (distributive) bargaining method.

Some would say that principled (integrative) bargaining is more idealistic, and positional (distributive) bargaining is more realistic. But what should be done if unable to choose between the two schools? Fortunately, for a more moderated approach, a middle path exists in the form of a blended "mixed motive" negotiation style combining elements of both. So there is, in theory and practice, something for everybody.

Case

North Korea, also referred to as the Democratic People's Republic of Korea (DPRK), represents an increasing security concern for the international community.

As brief history, in 1985, the DPRK signed the Nuclear Non-Proliferation Treaty (NPT). In 1994, North Korea and the United States signed the 1994 Agreed Framework, in which North Korea pledged to freeze and eventually dismantle its graphite-moderated nuclear reactors in exchange for international aid to build two new light-water nuclear reactors. In 2002, US President George W. Bush proclaimed North Korea as an "axis of evil" in his State of the Union address. In the same year, North Korea reactivated its five-megawatt nuclear reactor at its Yongbyon nuclear facility, capable of producing plutonium for weapons. In 2003, North Korea withdrew from the NPT, and then declared to the international community that it possessed nuclear weapons. In 2005, North Korea tentatively agreed to abandon its entire nuclear program, including its nuclear weapons, in exchange for energy assistance and economic cooperation from the United States, China, Japan, Russia, and South Korea. In 2006, North Korea claimed to have successfully tested its first nuclear weapon. This led the United Nations (UN) to impose what would be the beginning of a series of sanctions against the Stalinist state.

In 2007, North Korea signed an agreement at the Six-Party Talks stating that it would begin dismantling its nuclear weapons facilities, but then missed the subsequent deadline at the end of the same year. In 2009, North Korea announced it had conducted its second nuclear test. In 2013, after several non-successful negotiation attempts, North Korea conducted its third nuclear test. In 2015, North Korea state media claimed the country now had a hydrogen bomb among its nuclear arsenal, followed by a possible hydrogen bomb test. In 2017, North Korea claimed it had conducted its first successful test of an intercontinental ballistic missile (ICBM). North Korea subsequently conducted its sixth nuclear weapon test, causing a 6.3 magnitude seismic event, according to the US Geological Survey (USGS). North Korea thereafter threatened a nuclear strike on "the heart of the US."

Given the extremely tense nature and low-trust dynamic of the relationship between North Korea and the United States (among other countries), one method of applying a principled (integrative) bargaining model would be to seek and explore the shared and complementary interests underlying the seemingly disparate positions among the parties. This principled approach would be in stark contrast to the often-used positional bargaining model, whereby the parties state (and often restate) their proclaimed positions of "what" they want rather than "why" they want something. With ever-increasing hostile rhetoric, finding shared and complementary interests vis-a-vis the principled (integrative) bargaining model could lead to potentially positive and profound international security ramifications, ideally leading to a negotiation breakthrough whereby the parties "get to yes." In contrast, if instead the positional (distributive) bargaining model is envisioned and pursued, the tangible risk would be that such negotiation model would lead to continued suboptimal negotiated outcomes, or in the worst case, unilaterally or mutually assured destruction (MAD).

Given the high stakes involved at the highest level, encouraging policy pundits and political leaders to go beyond the positional (distributive) win-lose bargaining mind-set, and instead opt-in to pursue a principled (integrative) bargaining mind-set – by exploring shared and complementary interests toward a creative solution – may represent the biggest leap forward toward achieving sustainable peace in the Korean Peninsula and beyond. After all, the pursuit of happiness, safety, and security for current and future generations certainly are seemingly shared interests underlying the often intransigent and diametrically opposed positions related to nuclearization and denuclearization between North Korea, the United States, and the international community. Given such high stakes, using a principled bargaining approach may represent a seismic shift from "getting past yes" to "getting to yes."

Bibliography

Chang, R 2017, 'Hard Choices', *Journal of the American Philosophical Association*, vol. 3, no. 1, pp. 586–620. Available from: Cambridge University Press, Cambridge. [3 January 2018].

Fisher, R, & Ury, WL 2011, *Getting to Yes: Negotiating Agreement without Giving In*, Penguin Books, New York.

Lax, DA, & Sebenius, JK 2006, *3D Negotiation: Powerful Tools to Change the Game in Your Most Important Deals*, Harvard Business School Press, Boston.

Mehrabian, A 2017, *Nonverbal Communication*, Routledge Taylor & Francis Group, London.

Salacuse, J 2017, *The Importance of a Relationship in Negotiation*. Available from: www.pon.harvard.edu/daily/negotiation-training-daily/negotiate-relationships/. [10 December 2017].

Sander, FA, & Rubin, JZ 1988, 'Janus Quality of Negotiation: Dealmaking and Dispute Settlement', *Negotiation Journal*, vol. 4, no. 2, pp. 109-113. Available from: National Criminal Justice Reference Service. [22 November 2017].

Shonk, K 2017, *What Is Negotiation?* Available from: www.pon.harvard.edu/daily/negotiation-skills-daily/what-is-negotiation/. [18 December 2017].

Subramanian, G 2018, *What Is BATNA? How to Find Your Best Alternative to a Negotiated Agreement*. Available from: www.pon.harvard.edu/daily/batna/translate-your-batna-to-the-current-deal/. [19 December 2017].

Wiggins, C, & Lowry, L 2005, *Negotiation and Settlement Advocacy*, West Academic Publishing, St. Paul.

8 Reasonings
Making sense of nonsensical statements

Logic and logical lapses

The tendency of individuals to make sweeping generalizations in argumentation and rhetoric is the first example (of many examples to follow) involving logic and logical lapses in this section.

The first example is a hidden force called sweeping generalization. In sweeping generalizations, a general statement is made by an individual to a specific context that does not apply. An example of a sweeping generalization is the statement, "Artists are liberals. Andy is an artist. Therefore, Andy must be a liberal." To further illustrate this point, take the following statement as an example: "All library books are made of paper. Katie's kite is made of paper. Therefore, Katie's kite is a library book." While the former example may or may not have seemed outright illogical, the second statement may certainly be more striking in terms of understanding the scope of such a logical lapse (Damer 2008).

A rush to reach a conclusion can also be a sign that logic may have been violated. Hasty generalization (in Latin, *secundum quid*) exists when an individual makes an assumption based on invalid, incomplete, or untruthful information, often leading to a rapid-fire decision or conclusion. For example, the statement, "The battery battery in my new Tesla sedan had to be replaced after only one month. The obvious conclusion is that Tesla cars are just not well-built" (Walton 1996). In this case, logic should allow for the possibility that the owner's battery incident could be an unusual outlier case, and thus, not representative of all Tesla vehicles. Another example of hasty generalization is the statement, "Pete smokes a pack of cigarettes a day, and he is still as healthy as can be. What more proof do you need that smoking is good for you?!"

Another attempt at logical and rational choice in argumentation is a fallacy based on the assumption that a statement must be true simply because no evidence exists to prove the statement's falsity (no proof to disprove the assertion exists). This is known as an appeal to ignorance (in Latin, *argumentum id ignorantiam*). The illogical construct is, "A is not known to be true; therefore, A is true." Here, the proponent in an argument asserts A, and when prompted for the proponent's reasoning of A, the proponent then replies, why not A? (Walton 1996). An additional example of an appeal to ignorance could be the argument that, "Extraterrestrial aliens exist because no evidence exists that aliens do not exist."

Logic and rational choice may also be violated through bifurcation (colloquially referred to as the black-or-white or false-dilemma fallacy). With bifurcation, an argument is (often mistakenly) predicated on the assumption that only two options exist, such that, if A is false, then B must then be valid by default. Logic and rational choice should lead to rational thinking that more than the given options could exist as possible solutions to the problem. However, the two options provided are presented as the only viable options at the table. This lapse in logic and rational choice with the bifurcation fallacy is often exacerbated because of a tendency by individuals to oversimplify – sometimes to the point of extreme oversimplification – a complex matter into two starkly defined choices (Vleet 2012). An example of this would be the statement, "You are either with us, or against us." Similarly, "There are two types of people. Those who love their country. And those who are against it." Often in a real-world context, the options are not so starkly black or white as the speaker suggests, since the real landscape is composed of real complexities requiring nuanced analysis. However, the cognitive tendency to "think fast" and make rapid decisions in an increasingly complex and time-constrained world overloaded with information often gives rise to the allure of such oversimplification and bifurcation.

Logical flaws in persuasion can also exist through genetic fallacy, colloquially referred to as damning the source (in Latin, *argumentum ad hominem*, which is subdivided into abusive ad hominem and circumstantial ad hominem). The abusive ad hominem fallacy can be detected when an opponent to an argument criticizes or attacks the source of the original argument made, rather than analyzing and then criticizing the argument itself. The construct underlying genetic fallacy is, "Person A is arguing X. Person A is an idiot. Therefore, X cannot be true" (Dahlman & Reidhav 2011). Another illustration of the genetic fallacy in logic is, "The Conservatives favor cutting taxes for the rich, so you know an administration that hates the poor will be no good for average working folks like you and me. The party head is an extremist and elitist!"

Conversely, an argument that relies upon the veracity, expertise, or knowledge of an authority, when such authority is not an expert as it relates to the argument at hand, is a form of fallacy known as an appeal to authority. Here, the argument's proponent aims to add an irrelevant authority to add credibility to the claim being made (Hume 2004). The begging the question construct is as follows: According to Authority X, Y is true. Therefore, Y is true. An example of an appeal to authority can be seen in the statement, "My gym teacher told me that dinosaurs and humans walked the earth together. Therefore, dinosaurs and man walked the earth together during the same historical period." Another example would be if the legendary physicist, Stephen Hawking, proclaimed that the next trendy color among millennial fashionistas would be hot pink, followed by someone making the statement: "Stephen Hawking is such a super genius. So whatever he says is always true. It goes without saying, hot pink will undoubtedly be the next trendy color for millennial fashionistas!" In applying logic and rational analysis, it may admittedly be true that Hawking is a genius – in his area of expertise, theoretical physics – but this does not mean that he is a genius in all things, such as when it comes to millennial fashion trends.

Appealing to past behavior to determine future behavior represents another logical fault known as appeal to tradition (in Latin, *ad verecundiam*). In appeal to tradition, an individual's argument uses a particular tradition or custom to validate an argument, belief, or position. The underlying construct applying an appeal to past behavior is that particular things have always been done in the past in a certain way, as such, "Why change it?" The statement, "If it ain't broke, don't fix it" or "We have always eaten turkey meat at Thanksgiving dinner, so we will always eat turkey meat at Thanksgiving" typify this fallacy. Appeal to authority is widespread in its usage and application, and for this reason alone, it may not be as strikingly faulty in logic. Its logical and rational breakdown, however, is that a past behavior, action, or policy should not in and of itself provide reason to continue it (Vleet 2012). To illustrate this point, think of historical examples of when the appeal to past behavior was used to shape and dictate future behavior or policy on issues such as domestic violence, drunk driving, slavery, minority rights (women, disabled persons, children, the economically disenfranchised, religious minorities, and racial minorities, to name a few), and cruelty to animals.

Arguments to persuade others are also based on appealing to a large reference point in an effort to draw validity to the argument being made. Such fallacy is known as appealing to the crowd (in Latin, *argumentum ad populum*). Appeal to the crowd is a fallacy that often caters to a certain group based on similar, shared beliefs or values. The logical fault is that just because a group of people believe or hold credence to a particular belief system does not in and of itself ensure the veracity of such belief system (Vleet 2012). The following statement exemplifies appealing to the crowd: "The Democratic Party endorses Oprah Winfrey as its candidate for President of the United States. As a loyal Democrat, our duty is to support Oprah Winfrey!"

Deception in the form of misrepresenting a particular argument in a way that is distorted or exaggerated in a hyperbole is referred to as a straw man fallacy (Walton 1996; LaBossiere 2013). An example of the straw man fallacy is the statement: "You animal welfare and animal lover types want to give the same rights to all animals as to us humans. That is crazy. You people want to make eating all meat illegal. It is people like you who are ruining our country. And I will not stand for it!" Another example is, "Senator Vader demands that we should fund the Star Wars military defense initiative. I completely agree. Why would we want to leave our great land completely defenseless, vulnerable, and open to attack at any time by our enemies?"

Sometimes an argument based on an unproven and often unlikely set of events can represent logical lapses, in what is known as a slippery slope argument. Here, the fallacy is created when initial small, reasonable logical steps are then followed by a proffered chain of subsequent related events that then lead to a highly unlikely outcome (Lode 1999). The following statement exemplifies a slippery slope argument: "Allowing hate speech will start with extremists of every topic coming out of the woodwork, followed then by the persecution of innocent victims, and mass demonstrations that will imperil the state." Another example involves the following statement: "If voluntary euthanasia is legalized, then it will lead to involuntary euthanasia, where almost anyone could decide who lives and who does not." With such statements, albeit hyperbolic, it is clear that the extreme outcomes depicted do not necessarily follow the original premise. But in less hyberbolic form, such slippery slope statements can be more hidden, and difficult to discern.

Distortion and distraction is also an element in another logical fallacy known as a red herring (in Latin, *ignoratio elenchi*). Specifically, red herring is a fallacy made from a deliberate distraction in an effort to divert attention away from the original argument or issue at hand (Hurley 2011). An example of red herring can be found in the following:

> Politician A (Question): Did you have inappropriate funding relations with Organization X?
> Politician B (Answer): It depends on what you mean by "inappropriate," "funding," and "relations." So, I'm not exactly sure what you mean by your question. Even if I did, my memory may or may not be totally clear to recall at the level you are asking on this particular issue. What was your question about again . . . was it the popularity of my political programs that helped so many people get jobs?

Logic and rational choice generally follow a systematic process. Thus, when the logical construct underlying argumentation and rhetoric displays non-transitivity, this can be a sign of a logic fallacy known as begging the question (in Latin, *petitio principii*). Begging the question occurs when an argument is concluded without proving the argument's assumption, or alternatively, an argument's conclusion is based on an unstated or unverified assumption. The construct underlying begging the question is: Argument X assumes X to be true. Therefore, argument X is true (Walton 1996).

A classic example of begging the question is seen in the following dialog:

HAROLD: Did you hear that the new Smartphone X is coming out today?

KUMAR: Yeah, that would be totally cool to have one!

HAROLD: Everyone wants the new Smartphone X because it's the hottest new gadget on the market.

KUMAR: You should definitely get one then!

HAROLD: Definitely, but only after we get something to eat; I've got the munchies!

Circular construct can also exist in the form of tautology. Tautology appears in various contexts, in which a statement or argument made is essentially stating the same substantive content but restated with different wording akin to linguistic repackaging. Tautology is thus an argument that ends where it began. It is therefore viewed as empirically empty since it does not provide any new information (Peters 2001). Examples include statements such as, "It is either meant to be or it isn't." In such case, the sequencing is circular and not in conformity to logical construct. Even if the statement was similarly reworded as, "This final sentence is meant to be either logical or illogical," the statement would still constitute a fallacious fall – and thus, arguably not be fully logical or rational. Ergo, such reasoning would simply be unreasonable.

Case

On August 12, 2017, Elon Musk tweeted, "If you're not concerned about [artificial intelligence] AI safety, you should be. Vastly more risky than North Korea." The founder of Tesla and SpaceX also posted a poster photo with the words, "In the end, the machines will win."

Elon Musk – who has spearheaded electric vehicles and commercial space travel – is also the founder of OpenAI, a nonprofit that promotes the "safe" development of AI. Musk's thoughts on AI include the view that the global race for AI will invariably cause World War III. In Musk's view, AI represents a "fundamental risk to the existence of human civilization."

However, others in the tech industry do not share Musk's dystopian sentiments. For example, Bill Gates (Microsoft co-founder), in response to

Musk's "AI Apocalypse" warning, said he did not agree when he stated, "The so-called Control Problem that Elon [Musk] is worried about isn't something that people should feel is imminent. . . . We shouldn't panic about it."

One notable figure, however, who does agree with Musk is the famed theoretical physicist, Stephen Hawking, who is faculty at Cambridge University (UK). Hawking, who opines on areas outside of physics from time to time, has proclaimed that AI could surpass humans in just a few decades, suggesting, "Perhaps we should all stop for a moment and focus not only on making our AI better and more successful, but also for the benefit of humanity."

Such leading figures – Elon Musk, Bill Gates, and Stephen Hawking, who each have revolutionized their particular industries, such as in the electrification of cars, software operating systems, and theoretical physics – clearly require the highest of intellectual rigor. But is it logical (rational) in reasoning for us to appeal to their authority in the area of AI?

Some would argue yes, that the public and policy makers should appeal to their authority for advice on AI. Others, on the other hand, would counterargue no, that despite their obvious intelligence in their fields of specialization, that such high intelligence does not apply to all areas, and thus, does not necessarily equate to an expertise in the area of AI.

Here is a case in which the answer is not a starkly bifurcated yes or no, but various shades of gray. Given this, should the public, policy makers, and others be compelled to appeal to the authority of individuals – such as Elon Musk, Bill Gates, and Stephen Hawking – relating to the future of AI and its impact on humanity? According to some, the fate of humankind could depend on the answer.

Bibliography

Dahlman, C, & Reidhav, D 2011, 'Fallacies in Ad Hominem Arguments', *Legal Argumentation Theory: Cross-Disciplinary Perspectives*, vol. 3, no. 2, pp. 105–124. Available from: Springer Link. [8 January 2018].

Damer, TE 2008, *Attacking Faulty Reasoning: A Practical Guide to Fallacy-Free Arguments*, Cengage Learning, Boston.

Hume, D 2004, *An Enquiry Concerning Human Understanding*, Courier Corporation, North Chelmsford, MA. [2 January 2018].

Hurley, PJ 2011, *A Concise Introduction to Logic*, Cengage Learning, Boston.

LaBossiere, M 2013, *42 Fallacies*, CreateSpace Independent Publishing Platform.

Lode, E 1999, 'Slippery Slope Arguments and Legal Reasoning', *California Law Review*, vol. 87, no. 6, pp. 1469–1543. Available from: Jstor. [15 December 2017].

Peters, RH 2001, *A Critique for Ecology*, University of Cambridge Press, Cambridge.

Vleet, VJ 2012, *Informal Logical Fallacies*, University Press of America, Lanham.

Walton, D 1996, *Arguments from Ignorance*, Penn State University Press, University Park.

Index

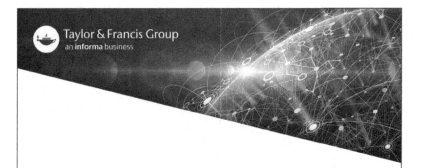

Printed in the United States
by Baker & Taylor Publisher Services